Praise for

Every Woman Should Know Her Options:
Invest Your Way to Financial Empowerment

"Laurie Itkin demystifies the world of finance so that women are no longer held hostage by a lack of understanding. She is her own best case study and proves to women that the power of information combined with action can be transformational. Stop being afraid about what you don't know and let The Options Lady lead you to financial freedom!"
—Ann marie Houghtailing, Founder,
Millionaire Girls' Movement

"This book stands out from all the others geared toward women because Laurie Itkin doesn't treat them like amateurs. She is bold enough to take them from the very basics to strategies used by the top male traders on Wall Street—and does it in an easy-to-understand way. And for that, it's a book worth reading for men as well."
—Jon Melloy, CEO, StockTwits.com

"Why follow Laurie Itkin's advice and invest a percentage of every paycheck? Because one day you may decide to shift your career path to something more fulfilling. When you have financial freedom, you can work at something you love without having to worry about money."
—Marney Reid, Founder, Stilettos on the Glass Ceiling

"*Every Woman Should Know Her Options* is a great roadmap for how women can utilize investor intelligence. Inspiring and enlightening, Laurie Itkin's story and advice to women is relevant to the present day financial landscape. Women no longer have to shy away from investment options they think are too complicated or risky. I strongly encourage you to read this book."

—McKenzie M. Slaughter, Founder & CEO,
Beauty and the Bull Magazine

"As entrepreneurs we are 100% invested in growing our businesses to the next level. *Every Woman Should Know Her Options* shows us why we must also invest in ourselves."

—Felena Hanson, Founder, Hera Hub

Every Woman Should Know Her Options

INVEST YOUR WAY TO
FINANCIAL EMPOWERMENT

LAURIE ITKIN
Founder, The Options Lady
Financial Advisor, Coastwise Capital Group

San Diego, California

Copyright © 2014 by Laurie Itkin.

Published by The Options Lady Press, San Diego, California.

Laurie Itkin is the Founder of The Options Lady and a financial advisor at Coastwise Capital Group, LLC, a Registered Investment Advisor. Ms. Itkin does not intend to provide personalized investment advice through this publication and does not represent that the securities or services discussed are suitable for any investor. Investors are advised not to rely on any information contained in the publication in the process of making a fully informed investment decision. Neither the author nor the publisher assumes liability for any losses that may be sustained by the use of information provided in this book, and any such liability is hereby expressly disclaimed.

This publication is designed to provide accurate and authoritative information in regard to the subject matter covered. It is sold with the understanding that neither the author nor the publisher is engaged in rendering legal, tax, or accounting service. If legal advice or other expert assistance is required, the services of a competent professional person should be sought.

Trading stocks and options involves risks and may not be suitable for everyone. Commissions, dividends, margins, taxes and other transaction charges have not been included in the examples. These costs can have a significant impact on expected returns and should be considered. Prior to buying or selling an option, investors must read a copy of "The Characteristics & Risks of Standardized Options," also known as the options disclosure document (ODD), which can be downloaded free of charge at: http://www.optionsclearing.com/about/publications/publication-listing.jsp.

Library of Congress Cataloging-in-Publication Data is available upon request.

ISBN 978-0-9913774-0-4

First Edition

Printed in the United States of America

Dedication

THIS BOOK IS DEDICATED TO my husband, Dan Clark, and my stepdaughter, Rachel Clark. They have always supported my passion for educating and empowering women to become financially independent through investing. Visualizing a 007 theme, Rachel designed The Options Lady's logo when she was just 15 years old.

I also dedicate this book to Hymen Weiss, my Pop-Pop, who died at the age of 97 in 2004. I thank him for turning me on to the *Wall Street Journal*, to which I have been a loyal subscriber for over 20 years, and for being my cheerleader as I built a path to financial empowerment.

Acknowledgments

THIS BOOK WOULD not have been possible without a number of people, many of whom participated in the editing process. First, I want to thank Scott Kyle for reviewing each chapter as I wrote it. Not only is Scott a brilliant portfolio manager, he's also an accomplished writer and editor. He was my toughest critic, and without his time and effort, this book wouldn't be at the level of quality it is. It was Jim Eliason who volunteered to review my manuscript early on and reminded me that although I was marketing this book to women, men would find it beneficial as well, so the tone of the book should reflect that. Melissa Stein provided strategic editorial recommendations and proved the book was persuasive when she informed me that after reading only two chapters, she decided she must put additional money in her Roth IRA! Frank Steele provided copy editing as the book approached the finish line.

Having never before worked with a graphic designer and not knowing what to expect, I was blown away with the quality of Milena Gavala's work and her passion for developing graphics that distill complex information into beautiful and effective visuals. Thanks to Michele DeFilippo and her team at 1106 Design for providing a suite of services, including cover design, inside layout, and brief articles and tips that took the mystery out of publishing. Hats off to John

Eggen and Jill Cheeks for the counsel they provided throughout the book writing process.

A couple of years ago Marc Covitt and I buddied up to attend several seminars and gatherings on options trading on our quest to find the holy grail of investment strategies. We spent lunch breaks and long commutes dissecting and scrutinizing all the potential risks of each strategy. When something seemed too good to be true, we got to the bottom of it. I recall Marc winning a candy bar for being the first out of 250 people to answer a quiz correctly. I came in third.

I am grateful to all the women who shared with me their personal stories of investment challenges and successes. All the vignettes are real, but in most cases I used false names in order to protect everyone's privacy. Special recognition goes to Becky Rudin for interviewing her friends and family for the bat mitzvah chapter and writing a blog post about her trading experience.

Finally, thanks to the team at TD Ameritrade who allowed me to take real-time data and screen shots of the *Trade Architect* platform and adapt them for the book.

Contents

Introduction

I T WAS SIX WEEKS before my wedding, and I was preparing a
spreadsheet that listed all my assets in support of the prenuptial
agreement my fiancé and I had agreed to sign. It was his second marriage and my first. Although it wasn't the most romantic of gestures,
we felt it was prudent.

There they were: the two individual brokerage accounts, the 401(k),
the traditional Individual Retirement Account (IRA), the Rollover IRA,
the Roth IRA, and the 529 college savings plan that I had established
for my soon-to-become stepdaughter. When combined, the balances
of each account added up to just over *one million dollars*.

I sat at my desk in a trance, staring at the document. I retraced
in my head all the actions I had taken over the past 15 years that got
me to this point. This was one of the proudest moments in my life,
yet I celebrated it privately. It was a sort of coming of age for me. Not
that long ago I was a 24-year-old woman who had bought 40 shares
of Starbucks with a $1,600 inheritance her poor Grandma Eda from
the Bronx had left her, and now I was 39-year-old millionaire about
to get married.

When I give speeches on investing in the stock market and the
use of conservative options strategies, I usually share my story of how
I built my own wealth. Everyone wants to know how I did it. After

all, they want to pick up tips and strategies in order to build their own wealth.

But what is more important than *how* I did it is *why* I did it, which I explain in chapter 1.

Women have a complex relationship with money. For many professional and accomplished women, money is the last frontier of empowerment. These women know how to control many aspects of their lives, but money remains elusive.

According to a 2012–2013 research study conducted by Prudential, *Financial Experience & Behaviors Among Women*,[1] "While women are more in control than ever of their finances, the study shows they are facing significant challenges when it comes to financial decision making and admit to a lack of knowledge about financial solutions that can help them."

The survey finds that in this economy, the majority of women (53%), including single, married, or with a partner, are the *primary breadwinners* in their households. Yet just 23% of these women feel "very well prepared" to make financial decisions compared with 45% of their male counterparts. Of the women who are primary breadwinners, only 10% feel "very knowledgeable" about financial products and services.

As I was reading the study, I was surprised to learn that well over one-third of women who are bringing home more bacon than their male partners admit to having little to no understanding of the very building blocks I personally used to achieve financial independence.

Achieving financial empowerment through investing was a highly significant milestone in my life, and my calling is to help thousands of other women reach the same summit. The reason I founded The

Options Lady (www.theoptionslady.com) was to educate and empower women of all ages to become successful investors. In this book I share my personal story, the stories of women who have grown and developed into successful investors, and strategies and guidance for you to also reach financial empowerment.

Chapter 1

How I Became A Millionaire Before I Turned 40

LIKE ANY TYPICAL CHILD, my mother received an allowance from her father. Unlike a typical child, she continued to receive that allowance for a very long time. How long? Until the year my grandfather died. He was 97.

My mother received financial support from her father because she couldn't make ends meet on her own. My mother divorced my father when I was four. Then my mother and stepfather divorced when I was ten. There was no man in the house for a few months, and soon thereafter came the string of boyfriends.

Of all my mother's boyfriends, I remember Robert the most. They were not together very long—perhaps a year or two—but he certainly made her happy during that short time. My mother seemed to feel proud and privileged to be his girlfriend. Robert was a handsome marketing executive with a major Pittsburgh department store who drank dry martinis and drove a Datsun 280ZX. He never moved in with us because he was still legally married to his wife, who lived in Florida.

When Robert was diagnosed with cancer, he moved back in with his wife and children to die. My mother told me after his death that he had "abandoned" her. I was only 14 and felt confused by the choice of words she used to describe her pain. She could have said she was "sad" or "lonely," but instead she used the word "abandon." I looked up the word in the dictionary and it meant that Robert had "ceased to support" her. I decided that I would never put myself in such a vulnerable, helpless situation, and from that point on, I vowed to support myself.

Robert's death sent my mother into a deep depression, and my brother and I were significantly affected. We yearned for a mother to nurture us, but at times she was emotionally unable to do so. I longed for my home to be a sanctuary, but concluded that would never happen; it was up to me to create my own sense of security.

I never wanted to end up dependent on a man for
financial security or for my sense of self-worth.

In high school I was motivated to get good grades in the most challenging courses offered and ace the Scholastic Aptitude Test (SAT). Through a combination of hard work and luck, I managed to get accepted to the undergraduate business program at the University of Pennsylvania's Wharton School. I wanted to pursue a business career because I equated "business" with "financial independence." I never wanted to end up dependent on a man for financial security or for my sense of self-worth.

I graduated in 1990 with a University of Pennsylvania diploma in hand, but no job offer. Eventually, I got my first job as a financial analyst with a small consulting firm through my friend, Renee, who had been my sorority "big sister." The job was in Washington, DC, required me to work 50 hours a week, and paid only $24,000 a year.

After sharing a house with ten roommates my senior year of college, I desperately needed a place of my own, but couldn't afford it. My mother's father ("Pop-Pop," as I called him) offered to pay me a monthly allowance just as he was doing for my mother. I accepted his offer, but I felt ashamed. He had already financed one-third of my college education—the amount that I needed after work-study income, grants, and loans. It wouldn't be until I was 31 years old that I would pay the last installments of my student loans.

My rent was $635 a month for a 440-square-foot, roach-infested studio apartment. Twice a week, I was awakened by the loud noise of the truck that collected the trash from the dumpster right below my window. Pop-Pop continued to send me a check for my rent every month. Then the unthinkable happened. I was laid off just three months into my first job. They said it was due to the poor economy. Nonetheless, I felt even more ashamed.

I found a new job not long afterward (which I would ultimately lose after a year), and received a starting salary $4,500 higher than my previous position. I called Pop-Pop with a big announcement: he no longer had to send me rent checks. I had developed a budget and was confident that I could live within my means without his support. Nonetheless, he insisted on sending me a monthly check. On the phone, I raised my voice and slowly said, "Pop-Pop, I appreciate your generosity, but it is no longer necessary." I could "hear" the sound of his face beaming. This was—and remains—one of the proudest moments of my life.

Pop-Pop was forced to drop out of high school to help his father support their family. He sacrificed his youth so that his younger half-brothers could stay in school and become doctors. As an adult, Pop-Pop became the owner of a small furniture store and was accustomed to working his tail off to support a wife and subsidize the lifestyle of my adult mother and her adult brother. Imagine his pride when at only 22 years old, his granddaughter was able to support herself.

For reasons I will never fully understand, my mother (who passed away at age 67) found it perfectly acceptable to be supported by her father well into her adulthood. Perhaps it was the era or the fact that she never married a wealthy man. She was a bright woman and worked as a literacy specialist, but she longed for a lifestyle that was grander than what she could afford on a teacher's salary. I think she felt entitled to living well and wanted to be "taken care of." I rejected that view and vowed early on to take care of myself.

When I first started dating, I never felt completely comfortable when a man treated me on a date. I knew I was equal to a man and wanted to be treated as an equal. Whereas most of my friends would complain about a man who insisted she go "Dutch," I actually preferred it.

My vow to become financially independent affected how I spent and saved money. I figured out early on that adopting a life of frugality would be necessary if I was going to stay out of debt and be financially fit. In contrast, my mother always knew that if she really wanted something—such as a down payment on a house, new furniture, new carpeting, new clothes or shoes—Pop-Pop would pay for it. I don't think he ever refused. Ironically, my mother never felt close to her father, and I believe that is because her role never evolved from dependent child to independent woman.

The $1,600 Inheritance That Started It All

Unlike my mother's parents, my grandparents on my father's side were poor. When my paternal grandmother died, she left me $1,600.

Although I wanted to spend that windfall on things that young women like to spend money on (such as clothes and shoes), I needed to begin investing for my future. At 24, I was currently employed but had already lost two jobs previously and concluded that I couldn't count on a job to provide financial stability. I had to build a financial cushion in case I was without a job in the future. Although Pop-Pop would be there to rescue me, I didn't want to rely on anyone but myself.

In thinking about where I would invest that $1,600, there was only one clear choice: the stock market. I recalled an eye-opening chart presented by Wharton professor Jeremy Siegel when I was studying finance that demonstrated that over the long run (despite its short-term risk) the stock market generated higher returns than other asset classes. Since I was only 24, I had quite a long time horizon and knew that stocks were the place I wanted to invest my cash.

In thinking about where I would invest that $1,600, there was only one clear choice: the stock market.

On January 23, 1993, I took my entire $1,600 inheritance and bought my first shares of stock. I chose Starbucks as my first investment and bought 40 shares at $39¾ per share. (Today, as a financial advisor, I would discourage anyone from putting all his or her eggs in one basket.)

There was no Internet as we now know it in the early '90s, so I was hungry for information. I bought a subscription to the *Wall Street Journal,* which I had delivered daily to my apartment. Although it was ten times more expensive than my *Glamour* magazine subscription, it ended up being a lucrative investment.

Believe it or not, I actually read from cover to cover the annual report Starbucks would send me in the mail each year. Back then, Starbucks would include a coupon in its annual report for one free tall drink of your choice. I remember walking into my local Starbucks store, handing over my coupon, and ordering a tall, non-fat cappuccino. When the barista asked for my name, I replied, "Shareholder."

The Three Most Important Financial Decisions I Made

Since I had been laid off from two finance jobs while still in my early 20s, friends and family suggested I go to graduate school for a master's degree in medicine, law, business, or mathematics. I was already carrying student loans for my undergraduate education and had nothing to my name (not even a car) but those 40 shares of Starbucks. Take on more debt and pay the opportunity cost of not working for income? No, I would get a job in a different field. Some in the family thought I had made a terrible mistake by not attending graduate school and that my future earning potential would be limited.

The *first* independent financial decision I made in my life was investing in the stock market as a young woman. The *second* was to choose to earn income *now*, instead of borrowing and hoping for higher income in the future.

I stayed in Washington, and my first non-finance job was in public policy. I became an entry-level policy analyst, asked for assignments that no one else wanted, and then was recruited at 27 to become an advisor to Oregon's governor because of the expertise I had developed in telecommunications policy. In the late '90s, I went back to the private sector, moved around the country several times, and rose up through the ranks as a corporate lobbyist for three publicly traded corporations. I ultimately ascended to the level of vice president—and never did I earn a graduate degree.

Just as I had dismissed the advice from my loved ones to go to graduate school, I dismissed the advice from the same people to buy real estate. Every time I moved I rented instead of bought. I remember the relief I felt when finally, at 31, I had paid off the last of my undergraduate student loans and was debt-free.

Although purchasing a house may be an appropriate investment decision for some people—especially those who plan to live in the same house for a long time—the so-called *American Dream* was not *my* dream. Why tie up thousands of dollars as a down payment in an illiquid asset, I thought, when I could rent and put all my income toward investing in the stock market instead of paying a mortgage? The decision to *rent* instead of *buy* was the third independent financial decision I made.

I recall people telling me how risky the stock market was and how real estate was a "much safer" investment. I suspect these people had never heard about **exchange-traded funds (ETFs)**. If I wanted exposure to the residential, commercial, or industrial real estate market, I could get it (and get better **diversification** while I was at it) by purchasing shares of a real estate sector ETF. And since ETFs trade like a stock, I could get in and out of my investment whenever I wanted.

The three decisions I made—1) buying stock instead of "stuff," 2) bypassing additional student debt, and 3) renting an apartment instead of buying a condominium—positively impacted the

An **ETF** is a "basket" of securities and typically holds stocks, bonds, or commodities. It might track a certain index, industry, or geographical sector.

Diversification is a technique that reduces risk by allocating investments among various assets. A portfolio of different kinds of investments may yield higher returns and pose lower risk than investing in just one asset.

amount of capital I had to invest in the stock market and the rate at which my money grew.

Live Small Now to Live Large Later

In my mid-30s I still lived like a college student. I had a table that I bought used for $10, on which I perched my television. Instead of feeling embarrassed when my boyfriend (now husband) came over, I saw this way of living as a badge of honor. If he had been looking for a "sugar mama," neither my apartment nor car would have provided any clues that I had any money.

At that point in my life it was more important for me to build my future than to spend for today. As a young woman, I already knew the difference between needs and wants. I began a self-imposed life course in which I would save up for what I needed, and I trained myself to minimize my wants. Of course I wanted the freedom to be able to treat myself to nice things someday, things like European vacations, monthly massages and pedicures, and membership in a fancy health club. I knew the time would come when I would be able to do that; what I didn't imagine was that it would happen so quickly, thanks to my commitment to the stock market.

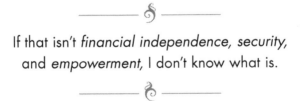

If that isn't *financial independence, security,* and *empowerment,* I don't know what is.

Unlike my friends with staggering credit card, auto, and mortgage debt, I don't blink when I have to spend money for an unexpected emergency. Whether it is hopping on a plane for a funeral, providing medical care for a sick pet, or paying an insurance deductible for a car accident, I don't have to borrow. If that isn't *financial independence, security,* and *empowerment,* I don't know what is.

Making the Most of My Money

Since I chose not to rack up new debt in the form of graduate school loans or a mortgage for a condo, not unsurprisingly I actually had money left over from my paycheck to invest in stocks!

When my company would give an annual bonus at work, my female colleagues would go on a shopping spree. I stayed home and bought more stock.

When my company would give an annual bonus at work, my female colleagues would go on a shopping spree. I stayed home and bought more stock.

Nearly every night I would log on to my computer to check on my investments. Although I didn't trade every day, sometimes I would sell stocks after they hit my percentage gain target, and other times I would sell stocks that had gone down in price, in order to free up capital to buy other stocks I felt had growth potential. There is no doubt in my mind that if I hadn't read the *Wall Street Journal* or a similar financial periodical every day, I wouldn't have been so successful. Sure, it took discipline, but it just became habit after a while.

As my career progressed and my annual earnings surpassed six figures, I added to my stock portfolio instead of spending money on things I didn't need. I maxed out my 401(k) and **Individual Retirement Account (IRA)**. Even when my income became too high to make a tax-deductible contribution to an IRA, I still contributed because the funds grew tax-deferred. In a tax-deferred account you don't have to pay taxes until you withdraw the money, typically when you are retired. As you will read in **chapter 2**, the use of tax-deferred accounts is a great way to accelerate the growth of your money.

There are many types of **IRA**s. The main advantage is that your investment earnings compound tax-deferred until you take out the money, typically at retirement. If you qualify, you can reduce your taxable income by contributing to certain types of IRAs.

When I maxed out on retirement vehicles, the leftover cash from my paycheck did not stay in my checking account or a low-interest savings account: I invested it in stocks and ETFs in a taxable brokerage account. Every December I would engage in tax-loss harvesting analysis in order to decide which losers to sell to offset gains from winners, and keep my tax bill low. Capital losses—securities sold for less than the original purchase price—can be used to offset capital gains on your tax return.

In addition, if your capital losses exceed your capital gains in any year, up to $3,000 can be used to reduce your taxable income. Any losses still left over are available for use in future years, without expiration. Tax-loss harvesting reduced how much money I paid Uncle Sam and kept more money in my account to grow.

Since money that sits in cash cannot grow into more money, I kept only enough money in my checking account to pay my expected bills for two months. I knew that if I needed money for an emergency, I could sell some stock and write a check or use an ATM card to withdraw funds from my brokerage account. I knew that in the worst case I could take out a margin loan against my assets if I didn't want to sell stock and realize capital gains. A loan from my brokerage firm using stocks as collateral would carry a lower interest rate than my credit card.

While most financial advisors (including myself) recommend individuals keep at least several months' worth of living expenses available in cash, I opted not to since I had no existing car loan, mortgage, or credit card debt. I had no immediate plans to have children or buy a house. If I had, I would have kept more money in cash. There is a balance between keeping enough money in cash to handle a layoff or unexpected expenses and keeping too much in cash that cannot be invested. Everyone must find the balance that is right for her.

She's Retired While the Rest of Us Are Still Working

My experience may not be common, but I'm certainly not an outlier. Take Lisa, 49, a retired CPA. She stopped working full-time this year after concluding that if she moved to a state with no income tax and a relatively low cost of living, she could live comfortably off her investments. Not dissimilar to my story, she started investing with a $10,000 work bonus and grew it over two decades—including the 2008 crash—to more than $1 million.

Like me, Lisa rented instead of owning. She chose not to fill her apartment with, as she calls it, "frivolous crap," adding, "Between makeup, shoes, and clothing, you can blow your money. I don't really deny myself anything, but I'm careful."

Lisa always maxed out her contributions to her 401(k) and never borrowed against it. She preferred investing in the stock market over real estate, because "the numbers never added up" to her.

Lisa never paid someone to manage her money and always felt more comfortable doing it herself. She would chat with friends and work colleagues in order to share ideas about stocks. Since mutual funds were the only investment choice in her 401(k), she made sure to check and rebalance her funds at regular intervals. During the 2008 stock market crash, it was critical that she didn't stick her head in the sand. In her brokerage account and IRA she traded individual stocks.

"You will never become a successful investor if you aren't willing to lose more than a dollar."

Lisa, 49, retired CPA

Some years Lisa's portfolio has fluctuated up or down by as much as 20%, and she is comfortable with that. It goes with the territory when you invest in the stock market for the long term. She warns other investors, "You will never become a successful investor if you aren't willing to lose more than a dollar." Lisa acknowledges there is some level of risk in investing, but says that "if you are thoughtful and deliberate, and check your accounts throughout the year," you can be successful.

Unlike most investors who dread a market **correction,** Lisa has been eagerly awaiting one so she can purchase shares of companies at bargain prices. Following her plan, she diligently sells stocks she thinks have gotten too frothy and takes

> A **correction** is typically defined as a temporary price decline of ten percent that interrupts an uptrend in the stock market. The duration is usually shorter than a recession.

modest gains. This allows her to convert some gains into cash, which is then available to buy stocks that get beaten down during a market downturn.

Retired before 50? I'd say Lisa's investing plan has been very successful.

Life throws things our way that we cannot control. But no matter where we start, there are small steps we can all take to invest for the future. Cut back a bit on what you spend and put that money you save into your employer-sponsored retirement plan or IRA. Consider renting a few years longer before taking on a mortgage. Spend a few minutes a day reading free online content such as *CNN Money* or *Yahoo Finance*. Find a mentor.

Once you have made the commitment to grow the money you have worked so hard to earn, you'll need to find an investment strategy that you understand and with which you feel comfortable. All investing carries some level of risk, and you need to be mentally and emotionally prepared for the rewards as well as the occasional disappointments. In the next chapter I explain why investing in the stock market (and ultimately learning how to apply risk-mitigation techniques) is such an important strategy for growing your money.

Chapter 2

What You Learned in 8th Grade Math Really Matters

W HEN MY STEPDAUGHTER, RACHEL, was young, she liked math. When she reached middle school, she hated math. One night, when she was struggling with her homework, she exclaimed, "Math is useless! Why do we have to learn this stuff?" I asked her not to give up on math, because although she might not realize it now, math has tons of practical applications.

Even baking a cake requires a mathematical formula. You need certain ingredients as your inputs and you also have to understand the ratio of how much flour to eggs, sugar, and butter is required. Since Rachel loved baking (and still does), one day I gave her a mathematical challenge. Since we only had two-thirds of the flour called for in the recipe for the chocolate molten lava cake she wanted to bake, I asked her if it would be possible to calculate how many eggs and how much sugar and butter would be required. She was so excited to eat cake that she figured out how to multiply all the ingredients by two-thirds *in her head!* Later, as we were biting into delicious pieces of chocolate heaven, I asked her, "So do you still think math is useless?"

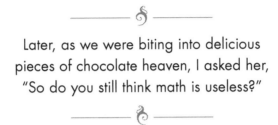

Later, as we were biting into delicious pieces of chocolate heaven, I asked her, "So do you still think math is useless?"

Unfortunately, girls who do not appreciate math while they are in school sometimes grow up to be women with dangerously little knowledge about personal finance and investing. Beth Caldwell, author of *Get Paid What You're Worth! A Guide For Professional Women*, tells her clients that if they start investing—even with a small amount of money—over time as they watch their money grow they will "suddenly have a newfound passion for math."

Bake a Sheet Cake of Wealth

Achieving wealth can be represented by a simple mathematical formula and requires fewer ingredients than a cake. For the basic "sheet cake of wealth," you need only three ingredients: *principal, **rate of return,*** and *time*. For example, if you were investing your money in a savings account, your principal would be the money you initially put in the account, and the rate of return would be the interest rate the bank pays you to keep your money there.

> The **rate of return** of an investment is the gain (or loss) over a specified period displayed as a percentage increase over the initial cost.

Let's take my $1,600 inheritance as an example. Had I invested that money in 1993 in a **certificate of deposit (CD)** that paid 4% annual interest (the average interest rate for one-year CDs during 1993)[2], one year later it would have been worth $1,664. It's a simple calculation: you multiply the principal by one plus the interest rate: $1,600 x (1.04) = $1,664. On its face, this "sheet cake of wealth" recipe is fairly simple. But factor in inflation and taxes, and suddenly your cake isn't very big.

> A **certificate of deposit (CD)** is a low-risk, low-return investment that ties up your money for a certain term, paying a slightly higher interest rate than a money market or savings account.

One Sunday afternoon in the late '70s while I was visiting my father, my stepmother showed me how to bake a Bundt cake using yellow cake mix, pistachio pudding, and orange juice. I brought the cake home that evening and told my older brother, who was eyeing the cake, not to eat any of it. On Monday morning I could hardly wait to take it into school. But when I tried to transfer the cake from the cooling rack to the platter, it fell apart. I discovered that someone had taken a utensil and entered the cake from the bottom underneath the cooling rack and scooped out an entire tunnel of cake! This is precisely what inflation and taxes can do to your wealth-building recipe.

In 1993 the inflation rate was about 3%, which would have left me with a 1% inflation-adjusted rate of return from my 4%-yielding CD. To make the situation worse, if the funds weren't invested in a tax-deferred retirement account, state and federal taxes would have been deducted.

To illustrate how inflation impacts savings, according to the U.S. Department of Labor's Bureau of Labor Statistics, in order to buy the same amount of goods and services in 2013 that my $1,600 could buy in 1993, you would need $2,590. Inflation is real and greatly affects your ability to achieve wealth. But just as you cannot control what ratio of flour to eggs makes a cake stay together, you cannot control the rate of inflation. So you need to invest your money in something with an interest rate (or return on investment) that exceeds the inflation rate.

The **S&P 500** is a stock market index based on 500 companies with the highest market capitalizations having common stock listed on the NYSE or NASDAQ. It currently includes Apple, Chevron, Exxon Mobil, Google, Procter & Gamble, and AT&T, among other major companies.

Interest and inflation rates do vary over time, but one asset class that consistently beats inflation over a long period of time is stocks. In 1993, for example, the stock market as measured by the **S&P 500** returned approximately 10%.[3] Over the past 25 years, the S&P 500 has returned, on average,[4] at least 8% a year.

Many women think they are being conservative by saving their money in a low-interest account: they are so afraid of another stock market crash and don't want to lose any money. The dark secret is that it is their *fear* of losing money that *causes* them to lose money.

During recent years, the interest rates on such products as savings accounts and CDs have been so low that the average interest rate is actually *lower* than the rate of inflation. In that case, you are actually losing money by investing in these supposedly "safe" investment vehicles. Gosh, it's not much better than stuffing it under your mattress. Many women think they are being conservative by saving their money in a low-interest account: they are so afraid of another stock market crash and don't want to lose any money. The dark secret is that it is their *fear* of losing money that *causes* them to lose money.

In addition to the inflation rate, you cannot control the tax rate either. You can, however, control where you invest your money. That's why it is so important to put money in tax-deferred retirement vehicles like 401(k) or 403(b) plans or IRAs. The money you invest is usually on a pre-tax basis and grows tax-deferred. In some cases you invest after-tax money (in a Roth IRA, for example), but it still compounds without having taxes removed while it is growing in the fund. With a Roth IRA you never have to pay taxes when you withdraw money for retirement.

Compound Interest: The Most Important Math Formula You Need to Know

Although it cannot be verified, there's a rumor that Albert Einstein called compound interest "the eighth wonder of the world." It still amazes me that such a powerful math formula is underappreciated by the masses. Most of us learned it in 8th grade and quickly forgot it.

Let's say you are 30 and are changing jobs. You have $20,000 in your 401(k) or 403(b) that you are now free to "roll" into an IRA (which is something I recommend most people do when they leave a job, because there are many more investment choices in an IRA). You have a 30-year time horizon in that you don't expect to withdraw from the account until you retire, which you estimate will be at 60. You are not sure how aggressive or conservative you want to be with your investments, so you model different scenarios using different rates of return. How much money will you have at age 60?

You can solve the mystery by using the compound interest formula, **B=p(1+r)^t**, which in my opinion is the most important math formula you will ever need to know. **B** is the balance (final amount), **p** is the principal (starting amount), **r** is the interest rate expressed as a decimal, and **t** is the time in years assuming that the interest rate is paid annually.

If you invest your $20,000 in an asset with an annual rate of return of 4%, in 30 years you'll have $66,260. However, if you invest in an asset with an annual rate of return of 8%, in 30 years you'll have $218,715!

In this example, let's assume no taxes are taken out while compounding is occurring because the money is in a tax-deferred account. While the formula looks simple, the impact it has on your money over time can be monumental. At first glance you might assume that after 30 years an investment with an 8% annual return would be worth double that of an investment with a 4% return. Surprise! Earning interest on previous interest enables your money to grow at an *exponential* rate. If you invest your $20,000 in an asset with an annual rate of return of 4%, in 30 years you'll have $66,260. However, if you invest in an asset with an annual rate of return of 8%, in 30 years you'll have $218,715!

Figure 1 is a graphic depiction of what happens when you invest $1,000 at different rates of return in a tax-deferred account. If you invest $1,000 in a portfolio averaging 5% a year, you end up with less than $3,000 after 20 years. In contrast, the same amount of money invested in a portfolio averaging 10% a year over the same time period would result in nearly $7,000. Although the 10% rate of return is double the 5% rate of return, the results are more than double due to the exponential impact of the compound interest formula.

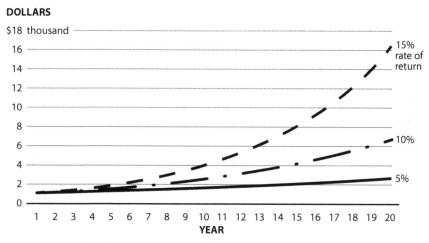

Figure 1: Growth of $1,000 in a tax-deferred account at different rates of return

Explosive Impact of Periodic Contributions

There is a much more complicated mathematical formula that you probably didn't learn in 8th grade that takes into account the impact of future periodic contributions; this is the recipe that transforms wealth from a "sheet cake" to a "towering layer cake." Thankfully, you don't need to memorize the formula because there are many free calculators available on the Internet. Think you can save an extra $50 per month to invest and want to see the difference if you save even $10 more a month? Want to experiment with different interest rates and time periods? Try the calculator at www.math.com—it's a lot of fun!

Put Inputs Here   Calculate Now!

Years	20
Percent Yield	8.0
Initial Balance	1600
Monthly Contribution	200

Results

Final Balance	125686.96

Figure 2: Savings Calculator
Source: http://www.math.com/students/calculators/source/compound.htm

Even small increases in this monthly contribution can
do wonders: that's why I ended up with $1,000,000
in 15 years instead of $125,000 in 20 years.

I started investing with $1,600 when I was 24, and **figure 2** shows
that I would have had more than $125,000 by the time I was 44 had
I invested in a diversified portfolio of stocks and added $200 every
month to that account. Even small increases in this monthly contribution can do wonders: that's why I ended up with $1,000,000 in 15
years instead of $125,000 in 20 years.

Back when I started investing, I don't recall ever seeing such
a chart, but I intuitively knew that if I added small amounts to my
accounts on a regular basis that the effect of compounding magic
would be exponential. So that's what I did. As my paycheck grew, I
consciously kept my standard of living about the same and put increas-
ingly higher contributions into that investment layer cake batter.

I didn't have much to start with, but I added regularly throughout the year and I chose domestic and international stocks and funds over **bonds** and CDs because I had a long time horizon. My monthly contributions when I started were much less than $200, and by the time I was in my mid-30s, they were much higher than $200. When I received bonuses at work, all of it went into the stock market.

> **Bonds** are known as fixed-income securities. When you purchase a bond, you are lending money to a corporate or government entity for a defined period of time at a fixed interest rate, which is typically paid every six months. Bonds with higher yields carry a higher risk of default than those with lower yields.

Asset Selection and Time Horizon

Over the 15-year period it took me to reach one million dollars, the S&P 500 returned on average over 8% annually. That takes into account the bear market of 2000–2002, when the annual returns were *negative* for three consecutive years. A person who invested $10,000 at the beginning of 2000 and needed her money three years later would not be happy. But in my case, this was money I wouldn't let myself touch for a long time. My goal was to grow it, and I was prepared to ride the hills and valleys of the stock market along the way. In order to obtain substantial investment returns, you must take on some level of risk and accept short-term declines. If someone promises you high returns with little to no risk, run for the hills.

If someone promises you high returns
with little to no risk, run for the hills.

The types of assets you buy should match your time horizon. For example, if you are 45 and are investing in a retirement account that you don't plan to access for 20 years, under most circumstances the vast majority of your holdings should be invested in stocks. However, if you are 30 and need to access your investment account within two years to cover a down payment on a house or expenses related to the arrival of twins, only a small portion of your funds should be invested in stocks. In cases where your investment objective is "capital preservation" versus "growth," less **volatile** securities such as bonds and cash-like instruments should be considered.

> **Volatility** is a measure of the amount that the price of a financial instrument can change in either direction—up or down.

It is quite common for investors to have different asset mixes for each of their accounts. For instance, a 30- or 40-something woman who left the corporate world to start her own business might need to draw monthly income from her taxable brokerage account. She cannot afford to take risks in order to attempt to secure high returns. Doing so might deplete the principal she needs to rely on in order to generate income to support her business. Such a woman might have a large portion of her account invested in bonds or cash-like instruments and only a small portion in stocks. However, she may also have an IRA that she will not access until she retires. For that account, a heavy stock allocation could very well be appropriate.

I often hear people—even investment professionals—make the statement that stocks are "riskier" than bonds. That statement is misleading and under many circumstances simply untrue. If you have a short time horizon, you might gravitate to bonds that have a low probability of default and yield a low return, because your goal is to preserve capital and stay even with inflation. However, that very same bond portfolio can be absolutely risky for a small retirement account that needs to grow larger over the next 15, 20, or 30 years. If you haven't invested in a manner that grows your money so you have enough to live on during retirement, isn't that risky?

If you haven't invested in a manner that grows your money so you have enough to live on during retirement, isn't that risky?

Overcoming the Fear of a Stock Market Crash

Many women I interviewed for this book shared with me their fear of another stock market crash. During my seminars when I ask who in the audience lost money in 2008, most of the hands in the room go up. If you were invested in a diversified basket of stocks—either through mutual funds, ETFs, or individual stocks—you might have seen the value of your portfolio drop anywhere between 30 and 40% during 2008. Some men and women I know pulled most, if not all, of their money out of stocks in 2008–2009, only to miss a major **bull market** which occurred during the following years. Because of fear, investors who enter the market with a long-term time horizon sometimes panic and sell even if they don't need the money. Many sell at or near the bottom—the very time at which they should be *buying* if they are long-term investors.

> If the trend of the market is up, it is a **bull market**. If the trend is down, it is a **bear market**. These terms are metaphors based on a bull thrusting its horns upward and a bear swiping its paws downward.

§

People are shocked when I tell them,
but had the 2008 market crash not
occurred, I would be poorer today.

I had approximately one million dollars invested in the stock market in 2007 right before the crash. Instead of running from the crash, I continued adding money to my portfolio as I had all along.

> A **dividend** is an amount of money paid regularly (typically quarterly) by a company to its shareholders.

> **Dollar-cost averaging** is the practice of investing the same amount of money in the same stock or fund consistently, regardless of the market price of that investment. It enables investors to buy more shares when prices are lower and fewer shares when prices are higher.

I kept investing in equities, but for the first time shunned hot "growth" stocks in favor of blue-chip, **dividend**-paying stocks. I figured now was the opportunity of a lifetime to invest in multinational, diversified conglomerates for 30 to 40% off. People are shocked when I tell them, but had the 2008 market crash not occurred, I would be poorer today. In 2008 the S&P 500 (including dividends) had a negative 37% return, but in 2009 it had a positive 26% return and in 2010 a positive 15% return. So although I was losing money on the existing stock I held in my account, at the same time I was buying new stock at a much lower price. This phenomenon is called **dollar-cost averaging**.

The Roth IRA Is Your Best Friend

I urge people whenever possible to establish and contribute to a Roth IRA. I call the Roth IRA a "super-duper savings account," because not only do your after-tax contributions and investment income compound tax-free, you also don't pay taxes when you withdraw the money in retirement. Although I do not recommend taking money out before retirement, if you do need access to the cash, you can take out the principal that you contributed—and on which taxes have already been paid—without penalty or paying additional taxes.

You can contribute to a Roth IRA in 2014 only if your adjusted gross income is less than $129,000 if single or $191,000 if married filing jointly. (The amount that you can contribute starts to phase out for singles earning more than $114,000 and couples earning more than $181,000.) In terms of dollar amounts, in 2014 you can contribute up to $5,500 or $6,500 if you are over 50.

If you are 25 and commit to contributing $5,500 every year that you would otherwise put into a savings account and invest it in a diversified portfolio of stocks, you have a good shot at growing the account to a million dollars by the time you turn 60. This assumes that the stock market will generate an 8% average annual return over the next 35 years.[5]

Since the stock market doesn't go up in a straight line, it is probable that some years your annual return may be negative. That happened between 2000–2002 and in 2008. However, if you are more risk-averse and invest your Roth IRA in a CD that pays on average only 2% annually, it is nearly impossible for that account to grow to a million dollars in your lifetime.

You Don't Need That Much Money to Get Started

Many women believe they simply do not have enough money to start investing. Don't let that stop you! My brokerage firm was very happy to take my $1,600 and exchange it for 40 shares of SBUX in my account. It wasn't particularly significant how much money I had when I started. The magic of compounding occurred because I took three actions: 1) invested in vehicles with high potential rates of return, 2) added small amounts of money incrementally, and 3) gave it time.

A **mutual fund** pools money from many investors and its manager purchases stocks, bonds, or other securities. Each investor has a stake in all its investments. Fees can vary from low to high depending on the type of fund and how you purchase it.

Although I typically recommend other investment options over **mutual funds** for a multitude of reasons, in the case of small accounts, they can be an effective vehicle. Many mutual funds allow you to periodically add small amounts of money without incurring additional transaction costs.

If you hold off on investing until you have saved a good chunk of money, you just may never start.

If you hold off on investing until you have saved a good chunk of money, you just may never start. And that I have seen over and over again. Recently a 55-year-old woman named Michelle told me she was "ready to start investing" for her retirement. She was excited to show me an old account statement that she hadn't looked at in years. Her money had been sitting in a money market fund (which currently earns close to zero in interest) and she had about $2,000 in it.

I was concerned for her. She was self-employed and told me she didn't anticipate having enough extra income to contribute to a retirement account. There was not much time to let compound interest do its thing, and unless she selected highly speculative or leveraged investments which could wipe her out, I couldn't see how investing in a diversified portfolio of stocks or bonds would generate enough money on which to retire. Frankly, it was heartbreaking. But had she started with that $2,000 when she was in her 20s and added just a little bit to it every month, it could have been a success story.

It's Not Over Just Because You Are 50

Lynda, 50, a legal secretary, found herself in a similar situation to Michelle. She had recently left her longtime profession to start her own business and a charity, and wondered how she would survive with such a low amount in retirement savings.

As a teenager, Lynda got pregnant and married the father of her child. When Lynda's second child was only four weeks old, she concluded she needed to leave her first husband. Soon after the separation, she started receiving notices from creditors. Her husband had run up credit card bills and spent money on drugs. In debt at only 22, she moved in with her parents. Her husband was a deadbeat dad: every time the government started garnishing his wages, he'd look for another job.

Lynda was just 20 when she first heard about something called a 401(k). The plan administrator at her job encouraged her to enroll in it. "I started contributing just $25 a month," says Lynda, a self-proclaimed "job hopper." Lynda started her career as a fast food worker and held a variety of jobs over the years, including bank teller, data entry clerk, booking clerk at the county jail, and a legal secretary at six different law firms. Although these funds were intended for retirement, Lynda never rolled her 401(k)s into an IRA or the 401(k) at her next employer. She would just pay the penalty and tax to the IRS and cash out the money.

At her last full-time job, Lynda was able to build up to contributing $700 a month to her 401(k) and was amazed at how the money just "snowballed" thanks to the employer match and the compound interest formula. Once again, however, she cashed out much of the 401(k) when she left to start her own business because she needed it to cover start-up costs. The remaining $43,000 she put into an annuity because she was "afraid to lose any money." When I explained to her how much her annual annuity payment in retirement would amount to, she realized it was peanuts. She strongly regrets those decisions now.

When planning for retirement, people often focus on how much they will have the day they retire. What they often overlook is how much they will need to live on for the remainder of their life and whether or not that account value will be sufficient.

The **Thrift Savings Plan (TSP)** is a retirement savings and investment plan for federal employees and members of the uniformed services. It is similar to a 401(k) plan for private sector employees.

Lynda's current husband is already retired and living off social security. Lynda recently made the difficult choice to leave the world of entrepreneurship and go back to work full-time as a judicial assistant for the federal appellate court system. This way she would have the security of a steady paycheck as well as a federal government match to her contributions to the **Thrift Savings Plan (TSP)**.

A few weeks ago I received a message from Lynda. She was excited to tell me that she had already started contributing to the TSP (through her first paycheck!) at her new job, and the match was quite generous. In just two months the account was already worth more than $2,000. She was already imagining how large it could grow if she kept making contributions.

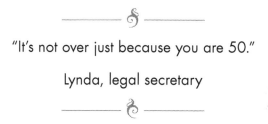

"It's not over just because you are 50."

Lynda, legal secretary

Lynda wanted me to share her story because, as she puts it, "It's not over just because you are 50."

Send Your Money Off With a Little Briefcase

Ellen, a 52-year-old jewelry designer, got married when she was only 17. Early in her marriage, Ellen recalls she earned less than double the minimum wage working in a record store while her husband held a union job, but with only part-time hours. She quickly figured out that her "Neiman Marcus" taste wasn't compatible with their "Kmart budget." It took a spendthrift husband, a few bounced-check fees, and an angry landlord expecting rent to be paid on time to force Ellen to seek a better understanding of money and why she should actively manage it.

While she was growing up, Ellen's father owned a few rental units. He would invest the rental income in the stock market. She recalls him buying stock in Ford. Although out of the house and married, Ellen thought that if she took an interest in the stock market, it might improve her relationship with her father. But when she approached him for advice on how to get a handle on her and her husband's debt problems, he was more interested in criticizing her lifestyle choices. So she turned to the library, bookstores, and trusted family and friends to learn how money works. She read biographies of self-made millionaires to see what advice she could glean.

"No one ever built a financial legacy
leaving their money under the mattress."

Ellen, jewelry designer

One of the ideas she embraced was to stop using credit cards and set up an emergency fund. When she needed money for an emergency, she borrowed from the fund and paid it back to herself instead of paying interest to the credit card company. According to Ellen, "Just the act of being debt-free when your credit card charges you 15% interest makes you richer by the same amount." Once she became debt-free and had savings, she needed to learn how to put that money to work. "No one ever built a financial legacy leaving their money under the mattress," she informed me.

Ellen wasn't sure if her marriage would last. Her husband had problems finding work, and since they had three kids to support, she hired him to work for her jewelry business. She is thankful that they didn't share any real estate investments, because when they eventually divorced, it was much easier to divide stocks than a house.

Naturally, don't assume your soon-to-be-ex-husband will take your investing advice. As Ellen recalls, "I told my husband while we were divorcing not to sell the Pixar stock he was getting, but of course he ignored my advice because he wanted the cash." She adds with an "I told you so" grin, "Of course, Disney bought Pixar a few months after that and he would have had quite a lot more money if he had just listened to me."

Ellen had bought Pixar stock after taking her kids to see the first *Toy Story* movie. It was the first children's movie that hadn't left her bored. She thought Steve Jobs was a genius. Ellen recommends that women get started investing by purchasing shares of stock in companies they think are well run and have growth potential. When she identifies such a company, she researches articles about the company and its management team. As a result of similar research, she recalls taking an interest in buying Home Depot, ironically just when her father was starting to sell his holdings.

Ellen thinks of investing like a garden: "Some folks just sit around and wait and see what grows up after last year amongst the weeds. Others plant rows of seeds they like, while others research the best fertilizers, amend the soil, and plant what grows best in their climate. These gardeners reap more because, although they are planting in the same earth, they invest time and effort to ensure their success."

Ellen gave her three kids the following advice when they started working and earning money: "Put that little suit and tie on your cash, hand it a briefcase, and send it to work!" You may find that with the application of basic math principles and sound investment strategies, your money can work just as hard for you.

Chapter 3

She Did *What* with Her Bat Mitzvah Money?

OCCASIONALLY, COLLEGE-AGE men and women attend one of my introductory investment seminars. I welcome their participation because I feel so strongly about motivating young people to start saving and investing early in their lives.

I attended one of the best undergraduate business schools in the country: the Wharton School of the University of Pennsylvania. When I was accepted to the school in 1986, our entering class had only a few hundred students, and females were heavily outnumbered by males.

The older I get, the more privileged I feel—especially as a woman—to have received such a phenomenal undergraduate education in finance. I studied urban fiscal policy, real estate finance, modern portfolio theory, monetary economics, and valuation of **stock options**. I think it is fair to say that most recent college graduates do not have this depth

> A **stock option** gives the holder the right, but not the obligation, to buy or sell shares of stock (or certain other securities) at a specified price on or before a specified date.

of education, much less the interest in studying it themselves as a hobby. Therefore, I was quite surprised the day I met Becky Rudin. After meeting a woman named Judy at my health club, I had invited her to attend my seminar, *An Allowance to Last a Lifetime*, but she sent her daughter Becky instead.

When I first met Judy, she told me that Becky ran a website called *The Sugar-Free Fairy: Making Magic with Special Diets* (www.sugar-freefairy.com). Since I had been gluten-free for about six months, I checked out the website and was impressed with its quality—both the writing and photography. It was quite an achievement for a young woman who had just turned 22. Becky's mother had also mentioned that Becky was interested in investing.

The day of the seminar, Becky stood out as the youngest attendee. She lingered long after most people had left. She then asked a question that stunned me, "How can I be you?" After all, Becky had graduated with a degree in psychology and a minor in sociology from a liberal arts college and was running a blog that any health-conscious, female "foodie" would be drawn to: *not the kind of woman you would expect to be interested in options trading.*

What Becky told me next really impressed me. She informed me that soon after her bat mitzvah she had invested the gift money she had received in a mutual fund, was annoyed with how little her money had grown over seven years, and was ready to become a more knowledgeable and active investor.

How many adolescent girls do you know who take monetary gifts and, instead of spending the money or putting it in a savings account, actually invest it?

For those of you not familiar with Jewish culture, the bat mitzvah typically occurs when a girl is 12 or 13, and it signifies she is entering adulthood and is morally and ethically responsible for her actions. Depending on the socio-economic demographic of the family, the gift money Jewish girls receive can be in the hundreds—or even tens of thousands—of dollars. In Becky's case, she had put her $5,000 in a savings account for a brief period of time before putting it into a mutual fund. How many adolescent girls do you know who take monetary gifts and, instead of spending the money or putting it in a savings account, actually invest it?

You Could Lose All Your Money!

A few months prior to meeting me, Becky had cashed out of her mutual fund and bought some shares of Tesla (TSLA), the company that makes sleek and speedy electric cars. Where Becky and I live in San Diego, these cars are popping up everywhere.

"The idea of letting my savings sit in a bank account earning less than 1% interest per year never sounded right to me."

Becky, owner, www.sugarfreefairy.com

During the summer of 2013, Becky wrote a blog post about her experience investing in TSLA:

"From a young age, friends and family had always warned me against the stock market. The instant responses when I expressed interest varied from, 'But you could lose all your money!' to 'Why don't you just put it in savings?' to an admonishing 'Stay away!' No one—not a single person—ever advised me to buy stock on my own.

"But my friends and family will also tell you that I have always had an ambitious entrepreneurial spirit. I do not settle for any less than I know I can achieve, so the idea of letting my savings sit in a bank account earning less than 1% interest per year never sounded right to me.

"So in 2006, I decided to put about $5,000 of my bat mitzvah money into a mutual fund, because that was the safest-sounding option that didn't leave my money just rotting away in a bank account. That's what I was told to do, anyway. I was a young teenager and didn't really do my own research or know what I was getting myself into, nor did I know anything about the fund, who was handling my money, or how I could access it. I was told to sit and wait and that it would grow, and that in several years it would be worth much more.

"I'm sure you can guess what happened next—in 2008, shortly after investing, the market tanked and I lost most of the money. But I couldn't see the money, so I didn't really feel the effects of the damage. I just remember being told, again, to sit and to wait, and that it would slowly but surely grow. And it did grow. In fact, it just reached its original value about a year ago, nearly six years after the initial investment, and then started gaining ground from there. I'd say that's a pretty bad return on a seven-year investment.

"I was tired of not controlling my own savings and of having to go through someone else to find out about *my* money. It made me anxious to think that my money was growing at such a slow rate and that I really had no control over it."

Quite the Ride

As Becky describes it, "TSLA was quite the ride for my first real dip into the stock market on my own. My boldness and deep curiosity about the stock market was rewarded astronomically by this investment." She acknowledges that she got extremely lucky with this investment, given how little she knew about stocks and the market at the time. Within the span of just a few days, she opened a trading account, transferred money, and bought shares of TSLA without doing very much digging. Becky reminds me of myself when I was also in my early 20s and put my entire $1,600 inheritance into only one stock: Starbucks.

Becky had doubled her investment in only a few months, and was getting accustomed to seeing the stock price increase every week. I explained that within the universe of stock investing, a home run in such a short period of time was an infrequent occurrence. I coached her about the concepts of risk and volatility and challenged her to imagine how she would feel—and what actions she would take—should the stock price begin to decline. I explained why it was so important to diversify and spread her money around, buying small chunks of stock in several companies that compete in different industries and global regions.

Becky was ambivalent for days, but ultimately decided to sell the majority of her TSLA shares. This action allowed her to not only recoup her original investment, but also lock in an excellent gain. She held on to her remaining shares in the stock.

Don't Lose Sleep over Your Stocks

One of the mistakes Becky feels she made was getting emotionally attached to her TSLA stock. She doubted her timing of the sale when she would see the stock continue to shoot up in price. She recalls, "Hardly sleeping all night after selling and locking in an excellent gain is certainly proof of that." Going forward, she wants to become less "emotionally" invested but more "financially" invested.

What I found so remarkable about Becky was that she didn't let her disappointment over the past several years discourage her from continuing to invest in the stock market. She wanted to find a better way and knew that if she learned some new strategies, she had the ability to be successful.

Could introducing young girls to the concept of investing help create a new generation of women who would become financially empowered?

A New Generation

Becky was now 22, and I wondered what her peer group was doing with regard to money a decade after *their* bat mitzvahs. Could it be possible that there was a correlation between what they did with their money back then (i.e., spend, donate, save, or invest) and what they did with their money in their early 20s? And if there was a correlation, could introducing young girls to the concept of investing help create a new generation of women who would become financially empowered?

Since Becky wanted to learn how to use stock options to have more control over her money than mutual funds and I wanted to know more about young women's views toward investing, we made a deal: I would teach her about options and she would interview friends and family for this book. Although she wouldn't have the time to engage in any large-scale, statistically valid sample, we both thought that the results of even a handful of interviews would be enlightening.

What Becky discovered during her interviews was discouraging. Although there were a couple of boys she knew who had invested their bar mitzvah money, she could find only one girl who had invested her bat mitzvah money. (The friend had asked her father to buy stock in Disney.)

Most of the girls had spent their money long ago. However, there was one girlfriend who had saved her money. In fact, she felt so strongly about *saving* her money that she admonished Becky for being "reckless" by *investing* hers in the stock market! But who is really being reckless here?

Saving Can Be a Losing Strategy

Despite a holding period that included the worst stock market crash since the Great Depression, Becky came out well ahead of her friend who was a "good saver." And at 22, Becky still has a lifetime of investing opportunities ahead of her!

> Despite a holding period that included the worst stock market crash since the Great Depression, Becky came out well ahead of her friend who was a "good saver."

As **figure 3** illustrates, assume on February 27, 2006, Becky invested $5,000 in a fund that mirrored the S&P 500 index. (For the chart I am using the SPY, a popular ETF that tracks the S&P 500 index.) *Even taking into account the losses during the 2008 crash*, seven years later (when Becky cashed out her mutual fund), Becky would have achieved more than an 18% gain on her investment, for a total of around $5,900. If her friend had saved $5,000 in an account generating 1% a year over the same period, she would have achieved about a

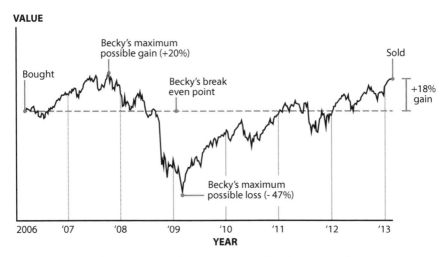

Figure 3: Price of SPY over Becky's seven year holding period
Source: Yahoo Finance

7% gain, for a total of less than $5,400. As discussed in the previous chapter, Becky's friend actually *lost* money because the interest rate she earned each year was less than the rate of inflation. According to the Bureau of Labor Statistics, you would need $5,792 in 2013 to equal the buying power of $5,000 in 2006. You can play with the calculator at www.bls.gov/data/inflation_calculator.htm.

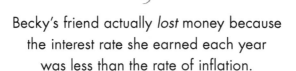

Becky's friend actually *lost* money because
the interest rate she earned each year
was less than the rate of inflation.

You can see from the chart that Becky was invested in the stock market during a particularly volatile time period. Stock market "corrections" happen often, as they are a regular part of the cycle, but the 2008 correction was one of the deepest since the Great Depression. Had Becky needed access to cash from her investment account sometime in 2008 or early 2009, she would have indeed suffered a loss on her principal while her friend would have achieved a small gain. That's why the stock market is particularly well suited for long-term investors.

Using the compound interest formula from the previous chapter, assuming both ladies continue on the path of their respective investing/savings strategies, who do you think might have more money in 10, 20, and 30 years from today?

Take Control of Your Money

What Becky learned at my seminar is that if she had invested her money in an ETF or individual stocks instead of a mutual fund, she might have had more control over her money and could have applied income-producing option strategies that would have served to partially offset the effect of the crash on her account. Certain options strategies (which I present in chapters 6 and 7) allow you to participate in the wealth-building potential of the stock market while "hedging" (or minimizing) risk. Is this easier than throwing your money into a mutual fund? No. But will it make you a more successful investor? I believe if you master the techniques, it will.

As I explain in chapter 9, you don't have to go it alone. There are money managers who specialize in using options strategies to generate income and hedge clients' portfolios if you want your money to be professionally managed. If you prefer to manage your own investments, the online brokerage firms that specialize in options have an abundance of resources to educate you.

Becky discovered that knowing exactly what was happening with her money was very empowering. She advises women to take an interest in how their money is invested, "Know where it is, how much you have, and what exactly it is doing." She adds, "If you don't like what kind of income or return it is generating and you are not happy with it, take action."

"Know where it is, how much you have, and what exactly it is doing. If you don't like what kind of income or return it is generating and you are not happy with it, take action."

Becky, owner, www.sugarfreefairy.com

Becky had the opportunity to learn about stocks and options this summer and is now working for a venture capital firm. A couple of her friends think it is very cool that she is dipping her toes into stock and options trading, while others react negatively, mostly out of fear and ignorance. Her parents are supportive and look forward to having their daughter mentor *them* about investing.

It is my hope that a new generation of girls (and boys!) will be educated to take control of their financial futures early in their lives and experience how empowering it can be.

Chapter 4

The Mutual Fund Menu

I AM NOT A BIG FAN of mutual funds, and that's why I had to include a chapter on them. For many people, their only experience with the stock market is through investing in mutual funds in their employer-provided 401(k) or 403(b) retirement plans. Although they might have fancy or confusing names, most mutual funds are typically a "basket" of stocks, bonds, cash-like instruments, or a combination of all three.

For me, mutual funds are like the guy I used to call when I didn't have a better date. Sure, it's better than eating a microwaved corn dog by myself while watching reruns of *Friends,* but it sure doesn't knock my socks off.

During my corporate career, I contributed as much as possible to my 401(k) for three reasons: 1) so I wouldn't have to pay taxes on all my income; 2) to receive "free" money in the form of the employer match, and 3) so my investments would grow tax-deferred. There was only one problem: my only choice of investment vehicles was mutual funds.

So why are mutual funds stuck in my craw?

Let's say you dine in a restaurant and notice the following on your check:

FIGURE 4: Example of Mutual Fund Fees

Maximum deferred sales charge (load)	1.00%
Management fees	0.60%
Distribution (12b-1) fees	0.75%
Other expenses	0.61%
Total	**2.96%**

You are probably thinking to yourself, "I already paid 25 bucks for the steak, 8% sales tax, and a 20% tip. What are these fees that are going to rack up another nearly 3% on my bill?" Oh, and the great part? Your waiter informs you that he will be charging you another 1% fee for recommending that steak over other items on the menu. Wouldn't you be better off finding a restaurant that serves a good steak but without all those extra fees?

When you invest in a mutual fund, you are paying some combination of fees of varying ranges. A percentage of the fee you pay compensates the team that is actively managing the fund's portfolio. Part of the fee may also compensate the sales force that markets the fund. If you have a financial advisor who manages your money for you (like the waiter in the previous example who manages—but does not cook—your meal), you may be paying a sales commission or another 1% or more "assets under management" fee.

Understanding Mutual Fund Fees

All mutual funds charge fees, and differences in seemingly small percentages can add up to beaucoup bucks over many years. What has always frustrated me is the amount of time it can take to compare funds. Not all funds charge the same fees, and even the same fund can be offered with different permutations of fees, known as "share classes." Although the information is available in a mutual fund's **prospectus**, which can be easily obtained at no charge on the mutual fund company's website, wading through it is tedious.

A **prospectus** is a disclosure document that describes a financial security for potential buyers.

The table in **figure 4** displays the combination and size of fees charged by a mutual fund offered by a large financial institution. (Not all mutual funds charge these fees, and some charge different fees.)

1. **Maximum deferred sales charge (load)**: May be assessed if a mutual fund investor sells her shares before a certain number of years have lapsed. The fee typically goes to the advisor, not the mutual fund company.
2. **Management fee**: Compensates the fund's portfolio management team.
3. **12b-1 fee**: Pays for the cost of marketing the fund and is sometimes used to pay mutual fund employee bonuses.
4. **Other expenses**: This is a catch-all category for miscellaneous administrative expenses.

There are many online tools that compare fees among funds. One of my favorites is the *Fund Analyzer* (http://apps.finra.org/fundanalyzer/1/fa.aspx), which is provided by the Financial Industry Regulatory Authority (FINRA). This tool illustrates the impact fees have on your mutual fund investments over time. The standard way to compare mutual fund fees is to look for the expense ratio that may be called "Total Annual Fund Operating Expenses." Although this will tell you which fund has lower recurring fees, you still have to factor in the impact of loads.

How Loads and Share Classes Work

When you buy mutual fund shares from a stockbroker or other financial advisor, you might have to pay loads (comparable to a commission), which are calculated as a percentage of the amount you invest. These loads compensate the advisor for selecting the investment for you. While some mutual funds are available only through advisors, my experience is that you can find comparable funds and purchase them through an online brokerage firm or directly from an investment company that offers funds. In many cases your transaction costs may be lower, because you don't have to compensate a human being.

The mutual fund industry has done something very clever: they get you on the front end, the back end, or in the middle through the invention of share classes:

1. **Class A** shares have a front-end load, which is a commission you pay at the time you buy the shares. If you invest $10,000 in a fund with a 5% front-end load, you would be buying $9,500 worth of shares and compensating your advisor to the tune of $500.

2. **Class B** shares have a back-end load, which typically decreases the longer you stay in the fund. This class of shares typically carries higher annual fees than Class A shares.

3. **Class C** shares impose a load every year you hold the fund. If you plan to hold the fund for many years, this may not be your best option.

There are funds that don't charge a load, and they are known as "no-load" funds. Investors often assume this means "no-fee," but these funds can charge other fees, in addition to the operating fees that all funds charge.

The bottom line is that your total return would be higher were it not for fees chipping away at your money. Over a period of many years, these fees add up and play a huge factor in how compounding works for you.

The bottom line is that your total return would be higher were it not for fees chipping away at your money.

Although some employers offer more variety for their employees, in the majority of employer-sponsored retirement plans, mutual funds are the only investment choice. That's why I strongly encourage clients who have left a job not to leave their assets there. Assets in a 401(k) or 403(b) can be transferred to a Rollover IRA in which individuals can continue to invest in mutual funds or a multitude of other assets such as ETFs, individual stocks, bonds, and—in some cases—even real estate.

Mutual Fund Investing Tips

In all fairness, mutual funds can be an appropriate vehicle to consider if you plan on adding small amounts of money to your account on a regular basis. Most mutual funds will let you purchase additional shares in very small increments without a sales charge. In contrast, if you were to invest $50 to buy shares of stock or an ETF and an online brokerage firm charged you $10 per trade, that commission would amount to 20% of your investment.

If mutual funds make it more enticing for people to continually invest the same amount (or more) of money every month, then

I'm all for them. When you take this action, you are conducting dollar-cost averaging, which as I explained in **chapter 3** means you buy more shares when the price is low and fewer shares when the price is high. Maintaining this disciplined approach is important and can be rewarding. My personal experience during 2008–2009 is a perfect example.

> An **index fund** attempts to track the performance of a certain index, such as the S&P 500 or the Dow Jones Industrial Average. It will own the same stocks that are represented in the index.

If you do decide to invest in mutual funds, make sure to stick to funds that have low expense ratios and other fees. You can also consider a special type of mutual fund called an **index fund**. An index fund attempts to mimic the performance of a particular index. For instance, a fund that tracks the S&P 500 index would own the same stocks as those within the S&P 500.

There is little sense in paying a stockbroker or financial advisor to purchase shares in a fund for you when you can typically find the same fund or something similar through an online brokerage account. The major online brokerage firms have screeners that help you sort through available mutual funds. For example, you can find the funds with the lowest fees, the highest ratings, or the asset allocation that most closely fits your time horizon and risk profile. It's like going on Match.com and narrowing down the field to three or four ideal dates. You can also go to the FINRA website I mentioned earlier and type in a mutual fund's five-character ticker symbol to compare its fees with other funds. Just as with any purchase, it pays to do your research and shop around.

If you have a stockbroker or financial advisor who recommends a particular fund, ask how she gets compensated for selling the fund.

You'll find out pretty quickly why you are being channeled to a certain financial firm's mutual funds over funds offered by the competition. Earning a sales commission by selling a product isn't inherently bad, but it can be contrary to your best interest if your advisor is profiting at your expense.

So now you understand why I'm not enthralled with mutual funds. What is the alternative for building a diversified portfolio? ETFs are an excellent choice, because they are traded like stocks and have one incredible advantage over mutual funds: options can be traded on them.

Chapter 5

Making Money from Stocks, Exchange-Traded Funds, and Options

Y OU MAY NOTICE THAT this book devotes several chapters to trading options (which are derivatives of stocks) without going into detail on how to trade stocks themselves. If you have never traded stocks or ETFs in an online brokerage account, you might want to get your hands on a copy of *Trading for Dummies*, by Michael Griffis and Lita Epstein. Despite the tongue-in-cheek name, the book is a comprehensive guide on how to trade stocks and ETFs. You can also cobble together much of the same information by searching online: I list several websites in **chapter 11**.

Many online brokerage firms offer tools to search for stocks based on criteria you choose. For example, you could search for stocks that pay a dividend greater than 2%, are trending up in price, and have buy ratings from several analysts. If you don't want to spend time researching stocks, you can subscribe to services that every week (or even every day) recommend particular stocks or ETFs and at what price to buy them (or sell if you already hold them). In addition, some brokerage firms provide free access to research reports and ratings of stocks. Although it is prudent to do your own research and determine how a specific stock or ETF might fit in your overall portfolio from a diversification standpoint, these reports can at least provide you with a starting point.

In addition to capital appreciation and dividend income, did you know there is a *third* way to make money when you buy stock?

If you already have some experience investing in stocks or ETFs, you are familiar with two ways you can make money when you buy them: 1) capital appreciation (which is a rise in the value of a stock due to its increase in market price); and 2) dividend income. In the first case, you make money from capital appreciation if you sell stock at a higher price than which you bought it. This is the old adage, "buy low, sell high." In the second case of dividend income, you make money if the stock goes up in price, but you also can make money if you sell the stock at the same price (or even slightly lower) than you bought it because you earned dividend income while you held the stock. If the dividend income is more than the loss of the stock, you can still come out ahead.

> An individual receives a **premium** when selling an option.

In addition to capital appreciation and dividend income, did you know there is a *third* way to make money when you buy stock? You can generate **premium** income by agreeing to sell stock you own at

58

a designated price sometime in the future. This strategy is called **covered call writing,** which is an option strategy I teach you how to implement in the next chapter.

> **Covered call writing** is an investment strategy in which you buy shares of stock (or use stock you already own) and then sell call options against that stock.

While dividend income is typically credited to your account only once every three months, you can set up your stock or ETF portfolio to generate premium income as often as every month, and in some cases every week! When Pop-Pop died and left my mother a small inheritance, she could have used this strategy to generate her own allowance to replace some or all of the allowance he used to give her. Instead, she had to sell stocks and bonds (greatly reducing her principal) every time she needed money, which made her very anxious. It appears that dividends and social security didn't meet her income needs, and it was very likely she would have run out of money had she lived much past her 67 years. If she were still alive, I know she would have benefited from reading this book.

The Four Basic Types of Options

As mentioned in **chapter 3**, an option is a contract to buy or sell a **security**—generally a stock, ETF, or index—at a specific price, called the "strike price." Unlike a carton of milk, which may be drinkable after its

> **Securities** are tradable financial instruments such as stocks and bonds.

expiration date, an option ceases to have any value after its expiration date. Most options expire on the third Saturday of every month.

Investors use options for a variety of reasons. For advanced traders, various combinations of the four building blocks of options can be constructed to suit very specific objectives. These combinations have fancy names such as "iron condor," "straddle," "strangle," and "broken-wing butterfly." The vast majority of this book's readers will never engage in these strategies, just as I have never used the hacksaw in my toolbox.

In **chapters 6 and 7**, I introduce you to two of the most conservative options strategies and explain why I believe most investors who take on risk by investing in the stock market should consider adding these options strategies to *reduce* that risk, with the added benefit of generating income. Before you read those chapters, however, you need to understand the four types of options. Options come in two varieties, **calls** and **puts**, and you can **buy** or **sell** either type. These terms may seem confusing at first, but just as if you were learning a new language, they will become familiar with time and practice. You can reference **figure 5** as a refresher at any time.

1. **Buy a call**. If you think a stock will *rise* in price, you might want to pay a premium to **buy** a **call** option. A call option gives the buyer the right (but not the obligation) to buy stock at a designated price before a specified expiration date.

2. **Buy a put**. If you think a stock will *fall* in price, you might want to pay a premium to **buy** a **put** option. A put option gives the buyer the right (but not the obligation) to sell stock at a designated price before a specified expiration date.

3. **Sell a call**. If you think a stock will *fall* in price, you might want to receive a premium to **sell** a **call** option which gives you the obligation—up to the expiration date—to sell stock at the strike price if the call option buyer exercises her right.

4. **Sell a put**. If you think a stock will *rise* in price, you might want to receive a premium to **sell** a **put** option which gives you the obligation—up to the expiration date—to buy stock at the strike price if the put option buyer exercises her right.

FIGURE 5: Buying and Selling Call and Put Options

Option Type	Description	Premium
Buy a Call	The right (but not the obligation) to buy stock at a designated price before a specified expiration date.	Pay
Buy a Put	The right (but not the obligation) to sell stock at a designated price before a specified expiration date.	Pay
Sell a Call	The obligation—up to the expiration date—to sell stock at the strike price if the call option buyer exercises her right.	Receive
Sell a Put	The obligation—up to the expiration date—to buy stock at the strike price if the put option buyer exercises her right.	Receive

Why Bother Learning How to Trade Options?

If you are already going to the trouble to spend the time and/or expense to identify stocks or ETFs that you think will go up in value, why limit yourself to the "buy and hold" strategies of capital appreciation and dividend income? Imagine if you were learning to play tennis and you were taught only two strokes: forehand down the line and backhand down the line. You already took the time to drive to the tennis court and warm up. Why not become a better tennis player by adding the crosscourt to your arsenal at the same time?

The truth is, no matter how much research one does, no one can *always* pick stocks that go up in price within a certain timeframe. It is the nature of stocks that they fluctuate in price. You will rarely see a five-year price chart where a stock goes up in a straight line. There are typically hills and valleys. If you are currently a stock investor, I'm willing to bet that if you look back in time, one or more of your stocks has stayed range-bound for months or even years. It can be quite frustrating. It is like living in a house and wanting to sell it, but you don't want to move until you can get a good price for it. Even more frustrating is when the stock price jumps around, but by the time you get around to selling it, it's back near the price at which you first bought it.

In the case of many heavily traded stocks and ETFs, you can leverage the potential ups and downs of stock prices to generate option premium and profit if the stock goes up, stays flat, or even drops somewhat.

How likely would it be for you to buy a property as an investment but do none of the work involved to ensure you have renters paying you monthly income? In the case of many heavily traded stocks and ETFs, you can leverage the potential ups and downs of stock prices to generate option premium and profit if the stock goes up, stays flat, or even drops somewhat. If you can profit in all of those situations, doesn't that increase your probabilities of success when you buy stock? If this intrigues you, then you'll love learning how to use options.

Often people tell me they are not interested in learning option strategies because they are buy-and-hold investors. I suspect what they really mean is they are buy-and-*ignore* investors. Even Warren Buffet, the king of buy and hold, doesn't hold all the stocks he buys forever. He is constantly on the lookout for companies he thinks are undervalued and he sells stock of companies he no longer wants to own. He has used options—specifically the sale of put options—to acquire stock "on sale," which I teach in **chapter 7**. Put options may be sold either as a way to generate income or to purchase stock at a discount (lower than the market price of the stock).

During the downturns of the dot-com bust around of the turn of this century and the 2008 crash, investors who effectively used income-generating option strategies to supplement their traditional stock-investing techniques had a briefcase of floatation devices to get them through those time periods without drowning. The income they generated served to offset some of the losses that legions of mutual fund and stock investors endured.

Wait! My Financial Advisor Told Me Options Were Risky!

When I tell people I trade options, the response I get most often is, "Be careful!"

Options have the unfair reputation of being considered riskier than other investment vehicles. As an example, in a 2004 book written by a well-respected duo of female financial advisors who cater to divorced and widowed women, there is a table that classifies types of investments. Whereas these women consider stocks to be moderate-risk investments, they include options in the high-risk category along with junk bonds, highly leveraged real estate, and penny stocks! I consider this classification misleading, if not inaccurate.

Although options can be risky when used for *speculative* purposes, the strategies I teach in the next two chapters employ options to reduce risk when investing in the stock market. Beyond that, they do a nice job of generating income that can be spent or reinvested to enhance returns. As Scott Kyle, CEO and Chief Investment Officer of Coastwise Capital Group, explains in his book, *The Power Curve: Smart*

Investing Using Dividends, Options, and the Magic of Compounding, "A knife in the hands of an ill-intended robber is dangerous; a blade in the palm of a talented surgeon can be lifesaving."[6]

"A knife in the hands of an ill-intended robber is dangerous; a blade in the palm of a talented surgeon can be lifesaving."

Scott G. Kyle, CEO & CIO,
Coastwise Capital Group, LLC

One situation in which buying an option may be considered "risky" is when a short-term trader buys calls or puts in order to speculate on the price movement of a stock (either up or down). Since one option contract typically controls 100 shares of stock, this leverage creates the opportunity for the return on investment to be high. But since options carry an expiration date, you can also lose your entire investment if you fail to predict the correct direction of stock movement, the size of the stock movement, and the time period the stock movement will occur. It is commonly known that 70% to 80% of all options purchased expire worthless, which can be bad news for option *buyers.* However, that's good news for option *sellers,* as generally sellers want the options to expire before they can be exercised.

Another risky strategy is selling a call option by itself (referred to as a "naked" call) because your losses—if you are wrong about your prediction—are theoretically unlimited. Even if you wanted to engage in this strategy, your broker probably would not give you permission to do so due to its undefined risk. Yet when you combine the sale of a call option with the purchase of stock (so the call option is no longer "naked" but "covered"), the very same call option (which is risky on its own) becomes part of a symbiotic relationship and serves to reduce the risk of your stock purchase.

Likewise, when you buy a put option, it can be considered a speculative strategy because you profit if the price of a stock *falls*. However, if you already own shares of a stock and you buy a put option to pair with that stock, the option functions as insurance. For example, if you hold stock and are worried that it might drop in price, and for whatever reason you do not want to sell the stock, you can buy a put option as a hedge. Depending on several factors, if the stock price falls, the put option you hold can go up in value.

The bottom line is that if you are already taking the risk of investing in the stock market, the two option strategies I teach in this book, if applied properly, will actually *reduce* your risk when investing in the stock market.

Many people are unaware that they can typically write covered calls and sell put options in an IRA. This is one of the reasons I encourage clients who have not done so to roll their old 401(k) or 403(b) into an IRA if they want to use these investment strategies. Options cannot be traded on mutual funds.

The bottom line is that if you are already taking the risk of investing in the stock market, the two option strategies I teach in this book, if applied properly, will actually *reduce* your risk when investing in the stock market.

Why It's Difficult to Find a Financial Advisor That Specializes in Options

As each year goes by, more and more financial advisors are integrating options into their portfolio management practices. Unfortunately, these advisors (I am one of them) remain in the minority. Call me cynical, but I have a few theories about why some financial advisors don't embrace options:

1.   Since one cannot trade options on mutual funds or annuities, those in the business of earning commissions from selling these products would naturally discourage the use of options.
2.   The vast majority of financial advisors do not know how to trade options.
3.   Overlaying and managing the sale of options on a diversified portfolio of stocks and/or ETFs requires significantly more time than putting a client's money in a cookie-cutter portfolio of stocks, bonds, and cash.

If you currently have a financial advisor or are shopping for one, ask what role options play in the firm's money management strategy. The response you receive (or the lack of one) will be quite telling.

A free resource I recommend to learn more about options is www.optionseducation.org, a website maintained by the Options Industry Council. There you will find written overviews and videos on demand explaining options and the myriad ways to use them.

Now the fun part begins! In the next two chapters I'm going to teach you how to generate income by "renting out" your stock and getting paid to wait to buy stock "on sale!"

Chapter 6

Writing Covered Calls: "Rent Out" Your Stock

A COMMON INVESTMENT STRATEGY is to buy a house or apartment and rent it out for income. Frankly, this idea never appealed to me because it just seemed like a lot of work. You have to find tenants, take care of maintenance issues, and deal with the bank.

My mother's third husband owned a few rental properties in a low-income section of Pittsburgh, Pennsylvania, the city where I grew up. Due to the law, it was difficult to evict tenants who were late on their rent. That meant that sometimes his assets were not generating income. I also remember how hard my mother worked to clean the apartments after tenants moved out. In one case—which I will never forget—either the tenants' dog had acrobatic skills or its owners had decided to "paint" a wall as a spiteful departing gesture.

If your goal is to generate supplemental income, then I encourage you to consider "renting out" your stock. It is so much easier, faster, and more convenient than dealing with real estate. You just need a computer, Internet connection, and some knowledge.

As explained in the previous chapter, the practice of selling call options against stock you already own is called covered call writing. A covered call consists of two steps: you buy shares of stock (or use stock you already own) and then sell call options against those shares of stock. You can use either stock or ETFs as the underlying security. A small percentage of financial advisors (including myself) specialize in this type of strategy, but it is also something you can learn to do on your own—with some education and coaching—in a self-directed brokerage account or IRA.

Looking at the big picture, it really doesn't matter if you generate streams of income from property or from shares of stock, as both are assets. My purpose here, however, is to clear up the notion that real estate is somehow *better* than stock because you can receive rental income.

Some people prefer real estate as an investment because they expect that over a long period of time, prices will go up—and they often do. But as with the stock market, the real estate market can be quite volatile. Depending on your time period, real estate values don't always go up. To make matters worse, when you decide to sell a property, there may not be a willing buyer. I'm sure you know at least one person (I know several) who lost his or her home to foreclosure and perhaps got into financial trouble by borrowing money in order to buy the home in the first place. (Leverage can be dangerous in the stock market too, if you use a margin loan to buy stock.)

Diversification Using Covered Calls

Besides not having to deal with tenants and toilets, another advantage of writing covered calls on stocks or ETFs rather than renting out real estate is that you can diversify risk by not putting all your eggs in one basket. Unless you are wealthy enough to buy a dozen different properties in various regions around the world, it is difficult to achieve diversification with real estate by itself. Yet in the stock market, because of the wide availability of ETFs representing a multitude of industries and geographic regions, you can achieve diversification with a lot less money. You only need 100 shares to write one call option. So in the case of a stock or ETF that trades at $50 a share, you would need $5,000 in order to write one covered call. With regard to some companies with high share prices, such as Apple, a recent innovation in the financial services industry has enabled investors to trade "mini-options" where the ratio is only 10 shares to one call option contract.

Writing covered calls is not a "get rich quick" strategy, but is an excellent way to generate income which you can spend or reinvest. If you like receiving dividend income from stocks, you'll love receiving premium income. As Scott Kyle writes in *The Power Curve*, "The use of options on top of dividend-paying stocks can be thought of as *equities on steroids*."[7] In addition, with covered call writing, you can generate income from many stocks that do not pay a dividend.

Buy and Hold versus Covered Call

Assume Brenda and Carol each buy 100 shares of ABC Company (ABC) at $50 per share. Carol, in addition to buying the stock, also sells one ABC call option with a $53 strike price. Immediately she receives a $100 premium for selling the call option, which is credited to her account. While both women made the same $5,000 investment for the stock, Carol in effect received a $100 "rebate." That means that Carol's

> **Cost basis** is the price of an asset which is used to determine your profit or loss when you sell it.

cost basis was lowered from $5,000 to $4,900. Carol can then use that $100 on anything she wants, just as she could with a product rebate.

Although Carol received income that Brenda did not, the trade-off is that Carol's maximum profit is capped at $400 no matter how much the stock goes up. That is because she must sell the stock at $53 per share if the call option buyer wants to purchase her stock any time before the option expires.

So which is the better strategy? Brenda's buy-and-hold strategy is the more profitable strategy *only* if ABC's stock price rises above $54 (see **figure 6**). If you have a strong conviction that a stock is going to move up in price by a significant amount within a fixed period of time, then you might want to buy stock without selling call options against it. However, do you ever really know how much a stock is going to increase in value within 30, 60, or 90 days? It would be like Brenda telling Carol, "I'm on a diet and I will definitely lose ten pounds

FIGURE 6: Profit/Loss for Buy and Hold vs. Covered Call

Stock Price at Expiration	BRENDA (Buy and Hold)	CAROL (Covered Call)	Difference
$56	$600	$400	–$200
55	500	400	–100
54	400	400	0
53	300	400	100
52	200	300	100
51	100	200	100
50	0	100	100
49	–100	0	100
48	–200	–100	100

within the next 30 days." Maybe Brenda does lose a few pounds over the month, but what if she falls many pounds short of ten? Or maybe Brenda does lose ten pounds, but it takes her a year to do it!

If you are the best stock picker in the world and your picks always go up, then stick with buy and hold. If not, you might be better served by writing covered calls. Your upside potential will be limited, but so will your downside risk.

Can you lose money trading covered calls? Absolutely, just as you can with any investment. Because you are first and foremost a holder of stock, if the value of the stock falls significantly, the loss from holding the stock will in many cases outweigh the gain you received from the option premium. That means you still have to do the work of any disciplined stock trader: you need to select high-quality stocks and ETFs that work together in a manner to create a diversified portfolio that reflects your risk-to-reward preference. However, since you also create downside protection by selling call options, you create a cushion you don't have when you simply buy stock.

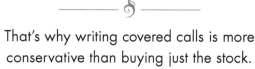

That's why writing covered calls is more conservative than buying just the stock.

In **figure 6**, while both Brenda and Carol lose money when ABC's stock price falls below their purchase price of $50, Carol always loses *less* money than Brenda, no matter how low the stock price falls. That's why writing covered calls is more conservative than buying just the stock. Interestingly, covered call writing is becoming increasingly popular with retirees, as low interest rates are causing bonds to generate less income than during previous decades. Since equities are generally considered more volatile than bonds, by choosing dividend-paying stocks and selling call options to generate additional income which can offset a loss in the stock price, people can invest in stocks in a more conservative and less volatile fashion. The next time a financial advisor or planner tells you options are riskier than investing in stock, lend her this book!

The Apple House

Now let's compare generating income from real estate with income from stock. Assume you bought a house for $525,000 as an investment. If someone offered to buy your house for $575,000 anytime over the next 12 months, you might be happy to sell it because you would have made a $50,000 profit, which is a 9.5% gain on your investment.

Suppose you could rent out this house for $2,000 per month (or $24,000 per year). Your annual rate of return is 4.6% if the market price of the house is the same at the end of the year and you don't end up selling it (24,000/525,000 = 4.6%). But if the house's value goes up by $50,000 and you have also captured the rental income of $24,000, your annual total return if you sell the house a year from now is 14%. Not too shabby.

But since this is a stock and not a house, you can generate a lot more income than just the dividend by selling call options against the stock.

Now, instead of owning a house that's worth $525,000, let's say you own 1,000 shares of Apple stock (AAPL) which is trading at $525 per share. Apple currently pays a quarterly dividend of $3.05 per share, which translates into a 2.35% annual yield on your investment. Assuming the company doesn't raise or lower its dividend payment over the next 12 months, since you own 1,000 shares, you would expect to receive about $12,200 in annual dividend income. This would be about half what you would receive compared to renting out the house in the previous example. But since this is a stock and not a house, you can generate a lot more income than just the dividend by selling call options against the stock.

When I write covered calls I typically sell options that expire between one and two months in the future. Looking at the AAPL option chain (**figure** 7), if you would agree to sell your AAPL stock

FIGURE 7: Example of Old Call Option Prices from Apple (AAPL) Option Chain

Expiration Date and Strike Price	Premium
AAPL Dec 21 2013 525 Short	12.25
AAPL Dec 21 2013 530 Short	10.05
AAPL Dec 21 2013 535 Short	8.10
AAPL Dec 21 2013 540 Short	6.50
AAPL Dec 21 2013 545 Short	5.15
AAPL Dec 21 2013 550 Short	4.05
AAPL Dec 21 2013 555 Short	3.20
AAPL Dec 21 2013 560 Short	2.51
AAPL Dec 21 2013 565 Short	1.98
AAPL Dec 21 2013 570 Short	1.56
AAPL Dec 21 2013 575 Short	1.27

Source: Data provided by TD Ameritrade

for $575 a share (a $50,000 gain, since you paid $525 a share) should it reach that price within the next 33 days (December 21, in this case), you would make $1.27 per share of call option premium—which would be deposited immediately in your account—for a total of $1,270 for the 1,000 shares you own during that period.

So what does this all mean? Since 33 days is a bit longer than a month, you can round down to $1,200 to estimate what your income would have been over a month. The monthly return from the option premium is then 1,200/525,000 or 0.2%. To extrapolate this value to an estimated annualized return, you would multiply that amount by 12 because there are 12 months in a year. You end up with an annualized return of 2.4% for the option premium *plus* the 2.35% for the dividend income. Altogether, you achieve income of 4.75% on your asset—which is roughly equal to what you generated by renting out the house—*but with considerably less time, effort, and hassle.*

Unlike rent that is sometimes paid late, the income from the sale of call options gets credited to your account right after your trade is executed!

Technically, you cannot accurately annualize this monthly figure because the premium you can secure each month will fluctuate due to a variety of factors that influence the price of the options you sell. Although I studied options pricing at Wharton and found it fascinating (I'm a self-proclaimed math geek), you do not need to learn the mathematical model. Just know that although the monthly income will be more or less some months, what you will receive is always known to you from the option chain *before* you make a trade. Unlike rent that is sometimes paid late, the income from the sale of call options gets credited to your account right after your trade is executed!

What happens if the stock doesn't reach $575 at expiration? In that case you keep the stock *as well as the call option premium* and can sell a new call option that expires the following month. If the stock falls materially below the price at which you bought the stock, choosing the next strike price and expiration date can be challenging, since the available call premiums might be much lower than what you want to receive. There are a number of strategies to consider at that point, and all have their pros and cons. If the stock does trade above $575 per share and stays above that level at expiration, it will likely be called away (meaning you will have to sell it at the agreed-upon strike price, even if the stock is trading at a higher price). That is still an excellent outcome, because not only did you bring in premium, but you also made a capital gain on your stock.

Here's where the covered call strategy really shines: because there are so many costs (as well as time) involved in purchasing and selling a home, you might not want to sell your house until it reaches a significant percentage gain. But since the commission for trading covered calls is insignificant when compared to real estate, you might consider selling your stock when it reaches as little as a 5% gain, or even lower. As illustrated in **figure 7**, you could generate $4,050 per month in income by selling the call option with the 550 strike price. If the buyer exercises her call option and your stock is called away, you can redeploy your capital into another investment opportunity. Experienced covered call writers know how to "roll" their options, buying back the initial option they sold and selling a new call option further out into the future, assuming they still like the stock.

This is the wonderful flexibility that covered call investors enjoy. Those who want to potentially profit from capital appreciation of the stock will write call options with strike prices far above the current price of the stock. Those who prefer to take less risk and give themselves higher current income and downside protection will sell call options with a strike price much closer to (and sometimes lower than) the current price of the stock.

Get Paid to Wait to Sell Your Stock

In certain cases, covered call writers will sell options *at or below* the current price of the stock. For example, if you think AAPL isn't going to increase in price much in the near future or if you are concerned that it might actually go down in price, one alternative could be to sell your shares at the price at which it is currently trading—$525 per share. By selling a call option near the price at which the stock is currently trading, you can get *paid to wait to sell* your stock. (In the case where you think a stock may be rapidly falling in value, it may be prudent not to wait and simply sell the stock without writing a call option against it.)

Looking at **figure 7**, you can see that if you agree to sell your shares at the very same price they are currently trading anytime until the option expires (33 days), you will get $12,250 in call option premium today, no matter what happens to the stock. This is one of my favorite strategies, and it doesn't seem intuitive at first. I know when I first heard about it, the light bulb that went off in my head practically exploded, and I couldn't wait to go home and write some **at-the-money** call options on my stock.

> An **at-the-money** option is one where the strike price is the same (or close to it) as the price of the underlying security.

A variation of covered call writing is to buy shares of stock and sell call options immediately. Most brokers allow you to do this in one transaction, sometimes called a "buy write." In effect, you lower your cost basis on the stock because you receive immediate income that offsets the purchase price of the stock. You might do this to provide a cushion in case the stock falls in price after you buy it. You control how much potential capital appreciation you give up in exchange for different levels of cushion. In **figure 8**, you can see that if you write a covered call with a 525 strike price, after accounting for the immediate income you receive from the call option, the stock that costs $525 a share will in effect cost you less than $511 a share.

FIGURE 8: Example of Old Covered Call Prices from Apple (AAPL) Option Chain

Strike Price	Open
AAPL 525 Covered Call	510.91
AAPL 530 Covered Call	513.11
AAPL 535 Covered Call	515.06
AAPL 540 Covered Call	516.66
AAPL 545 Covered Call	518.11
AAPL 550 Covered Call	519.21
AAPL 555 Covered Call	520.11
AAPL 560 Covered Call	520.80
AAPL 565 Covered Call	521.34
AAPL 570 Covered Call	521.76

Source: Data provided by TD Ameritrade

Covered Calls for Supplemental Income

When I first started my one-on-one coaching service for self-directed investors, I anticipated that the clients who would quickly grasp the covered call concept would be engineers, scientists, and accountants—anyone with expertise in math and analysis. However, I have been routinely surprised by how quickly some of the women who work outside those fields master the subject. I'm sure my teaching style has something to do with it, but I like to think it provides evidence that trading of options isn't just for "math geeks" and that it can be mastered by women who come with one simple attribute—a desire to learn.

Vessa, 49, is an intuitive counsel and trains others to become clairvoyant—not your typical "number-cruncher." Yet every time I meet with her, she has her portfolio up on the computer and a calculator nearby ready to compute some "what-if" scenarios based on various strike prices and time horizons we explore together. She had heard about options but hadn't yet ventured beyond trading stocks in her self-directed brokerage and Roth IRA accounts. That all changed when my neighbor asked me to donate a free coaching session for a fundraiser for her daughter's elementary school (which also happened to be Vessa's son's school), and she and her husband bid on and won the session.

As is typical of many couples I meet, Vessa and her husband had different risk tolerances and time horizons. He was interested in learning how to use options in a speculative way to make a quick gain by betting that a certain stock was overvalued and would quickly fall in price, while she was interested in using options to generate steady income from the stocks she already owned and to make her portfolio *less* speculative.

Back when Vessa and her sister were teenagers, they resisted when their mother tried to teach them about the stock market. Their mother, educated and trained as a chemist, became a stockbroker as a second career and had wanted the girls to grow up to be financially independent. When Vessa's mother died and she and her sister inherited their mother's stocks, neither knew what to do with them. They were referred to a stock broker who ended up managing their portfolios. Vessa and her sister took different routes from there; Vessa kept some money with the stock broker and at the same time started to build her own stock portfolio, while her sister eventually sold the stocks from her inheritance and cashed out.

Not knowing where to start, Vessa decided to attend a wealth-building seminar and heard David Bach's famous advice, "Pay yourself first," which really resonated with her. Since she was self-employed with no employer-provided retirement plan, she decided to open a Roth IRA as well as a taxable brokerage account. She then started asking others what stocks they owned. At her tennis club, none of the women seemed to know the first thing about investing, so she turned to the older men. She recalls being told to buy Qualcomm (QCOM), Sun Microsystems (SUN), and Intel (INTC). She began trading stocks with only $8,000 in her brokerage account, which over time grew to $60,000 because not only did her stocks generally go up in price—she continued to add money to her accounts. Anytime she saw spare cash in her checking account, she would transfer it to her Roth IRA. When she maxed out her Roth IRA for the year, she would add money to her brokerage account. During years her business wasn't making much money, she would cut back on spending instead of pulling funds from her brokerage account.

Vessa was very fortunate to hold QCOM in her portfolio during 1999, as the share price grew exponentially. Before the high tech bubble burst in 2000, she had already sold half her stock to use as a down payment on a property she planned to rent out for income. That property turned out to be a good investment.

Soon after, when Vessa got married, she and her husband bought a four-bedroom house in which to live. "Then we bought a third house with gains from more of my stock," Vessa explained to me. "We thought we would flip it in two years and make $200,000, but instead, the housing market crashed and the payment kept going up: first it was $2,300, then $2,600, then $2,900, then $3,300, then $3,900, then $4,400." Vessa couldn't persuade the bank to refinance the loan even though she called the bank every month and also later hired a lawyer to help her. "We were only receiving $2,400 a month in rent," she told me. In 2003 the couple went through a foreclosure and Vessa laments that she ruined her and her husband's credit rating.

Once she learned that she didn't need to invest
in real estate in order to generate income,
she became a covered-call convert.

Despite losing money on that investment, Vessa slowly built her stock portfolio back up. Once she learned that she didn't need to invest in real estate in order to generate income, she became a covered-call convert.

During the strong bull market of 2013, there were times when the price of the stock she bought exceeded the strike price and was called away. While sometimes she wished she had not sold the call option which capped her upside gain potential, there were times when the price of certain stocks stayed flat or even decreased in value, and she is glad she sold call options. She decided to sign up for another three-session coaching package with me so she could learn advanced covered call strategies such as how to "roll" her call options to the next month instead of letting them expire, as well as other management strategies.

One of the reasons Vessa never took an interest in the stock market as a child was her mother's approach; she didn't make it fun to learn. Vessa is teaching her eight-year-old son by engaging him. When he finds a product he likes, Vessa and he research the company that makes it. Sometimes she allows him to buy one share of the company in *his* brokerage account. He sits on her lap and she tells him which buttons to press.

> One way for a parent to establish a brokerage account for a child is by opening a **Uniform Transfer to Minors Account (UTMA)**. The adult is the custodian of the account until the child reaches 18 or 21, depending on the state.

At the table this past Thanksgiving, Vessa's son was bragging to his extended family that he owns one share of McDonald's. He even impressed everyone by informing them what the stock symbol is: MCD. He also owns Target, but sold his Radio Shack when the price of the stock went down. Vessa's mother would be so proud of her grandson.

So now you know how to generate income from your stock by writing covered calls. In the next chapter I'm going to teach you how you can get paid to wait to buy stock "on sale" by selling put options.

Chapter 7

Selling Puts: Get Paid to Wait to Buy Stock "On Sale"

IMAGINE SPOTTING A PAIR OF $200 stilettos at your favorite store. You love them and want to buy them. However, you know that the store often runs sales and there is a good chance that if you come back a month later, the stilettos will be marked down by 10%. You don't need the stilettos right away, and of course you would prefer to pay $180 instead of $200. So instead of buying them today, you set aside $180 (that you won't spend on anything else) and come back a month later to buy the shoes.

What's more fun than buying a new pair of shoes? Getting them on sale! And what could possibly be more fun than that? Getting paid to wait until they go on sale! Wouldn't it be marvelous if the store offered you five bucks in cash today if you commit to coming back a month from now and purchasing the shoes for $180? And here's the kicker: if you come back in a month and the shoes are not marked down at least 10%, you no longer have the obligation to buy the shoes, yet you *get to keep* the five bucks.

There is one important condition: if the shoes are marked down more than 10% anytime during the month, the store can call you and ask you to come in and fork over $180 for shoes that might now be selling for *less* than $180. You have to hold up your end of the bargain, which is to pay $180 for the shoes while keeping the five bucks they initially paid you. Even if this happened, isn't your wallet in better shape than your friends who couldn't resist and paid retail price ($200) for the shoes?

I doubt you could secure shoes this way if you walked into Macy's, but it happens all the time with shares of stock.

Limit Orders

Some traders use **limit orders** to purchase stock at a discount. If the stock is currently trading at $200 per share (like the stilettos), a trader may set a limit order to purchase shares at a lower price, such as $180. She likes the stock and wants to own it, but thinks she can get a better deal if she waits.

> A **limit order** is an order to buy or sell a stock at a specified price or better.

But what if the stock never falls in value to hit that lower price? The trader never acquires the stock and she gets nothing in return for tying up her capital waiting for the stock to "go on sale." She has to keep cash available in her account while she waits for the price of the stock to fall from $200 to $180 so she can buy the shares.

> When you sell one **cash-secured put option**, you receive a premium and must have enough cash in your account to purchase 100 shares of stock at the strike price until expiration of the option.

Sell a Put Option and Get Paid to Wait

When I first learned how to sell a **cash-secured put option**, I just couldn't believe it! There was actually a way *to get paid* while I was waiting to potentially purchase stock at a lower price. Why was this secret kept from me for all those years? Although I had studied the pricing of options in college, I was never taught how to apply the subject of options in a practical sense to build my wealth. Discovering this juicy secret solved a big problem for me: I would now be able to get a return on my capital while it was sitting around, waiting to buy stock.

Discovering this juicy secret solved a big problem for me: I would now be able to get a return on my capital while it was sitting around, waiting to buy stock.

In keeping with the shoe analogy, let's now look at athletic shoes. One publicly traded company that sells a lot of shoes is Nike (NKE). At the time of this writing, NKE was trading at $71.94 per share. I could buy the stock outright at the market price. Or, if I like the stock but don't want to pay more than $70 for it, I could set a limit order to purchase shares if and when it drops to $70. But if I desire to purchase at least 100 shares of NKE, I could sell a put option with a strike price of $70.

Assume I do not have an account that allows me to trade on margin or I am trading within my IRA. If I place a limit order to buy 100 shares of NKE at $70 a share, I have to allocate $7,000 that can't be used for other purposes so that I have money available to purchase the shares if they fall to meet my limit price.

If there is one thing I don't like, it's keeping lots of cash lying around without getting a return on it. As I stated earlier, when you place a limit order, you are not getting a return on your money, except perhaps a tiny amount of interest. When I sell a put option (instead of placing a limit order), I am getting paid a return on my cash as I wait to buy the stock at a lower price, should it be "put" to me.

Using the NKE example, instead of buying 100 shares of stock outright at $71.94 a share, or placing a limit order at $70, I could sell a put option with a strike price of $70 and choose an expiration date sometime in the future. Typically, I sell a put option with an expiration of between 30 and 60 days.

As displayed in the NKE option chain (**figure 9**), if I sell the $70 put option with an expiration date of November 16 (which is 30 days from today), I will receive a premium of $121. This is immediate income in my account. Contrast that with a limit order, where I receive nothing.

FIGURE 9: Example of Old Put Option Prices from Nike (NKE) Option Chain

Expiration Date and Strike Price	Premium
NKE Nov 16 2013 65 Short Put	0.32
NKE Nov 16 2013 67.5 Short Put	0.62
NKE Nov 16 2013 70 Short Put	**1.21**
NKE Nov 16 2013 72.5 Short Put	2.23
NKE Nov 16 2013 75 Short Put	3.75
NKE Nov 16 2013 77.5 Short Put	5.70
NKE Nov 16 2013 80 Short Put	7.95

Source: Data provided by TD Ameritrade

As a reminder, each option contract controls 100 shares of stock. That's why the 1.21 per put shown in the chart translates into $121 in my pocket. (I can sell two put options if I am prepared to potentially purchase 200 shares of stock.)

In exchange for the $121 premium, I have an obligation to purchase 100 shares of NKE at $70 a share if the price of NKE stock declines and the shares are "put" to me anytime over the next 30 days. It is likely that the put option *buyer* would want me to purchase the shares at $70 if the stock was trading *lower* than $70 when the put option expires on November 16. If the stock is trading *above* $70 at expiration, the buyer won't sell the stock to me for $70 per share.

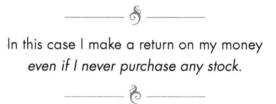

In this case I make a return on my money
even if I never purchase any stock.

If the stock trades above $70 per share at expiration, the put option expires worthless. In that case, I keep my $121 and don't have to take ownership of the stock. I don't have to do anything at all, or I can use the cash I have been holding and allocate it to a different investment. In this case I make a return on my money *even if I never purchase any stock.*

Think about this for a moment: The $121 is mine to keep if the stock goes up, stays flat, or even drops below $71.94 per share. What a powerful outcome!

My break-even point (the point at which I no longer have a gain) on this trade is $68.79 ($70–$1.21). If I had simply bought the stock outright at $71.94 per share and it fell to $68.79, my loss would be

$3.15 per share, or $315 on 100 shares. But if I sold the put option with the $70 strike price and the stock fell to $68.79, I would be breakeven on the trade. Had I bought the stock at $71.94 and it fell to $70.94, I would have lost $100 on the trade. But if I sold the $70 put, I would gain $121 on the trade.

The only situation in which I'm better off if I buy the stock outright versus selling a put option is if NKE increases from $71.94 to more than $73.15 at the end of 30 days.[8]

In effect, I am exchanging *potential capital gains* based on appreciation of the stock for *guaranteed income* today and the potential to buy stock at a lower entry point. That's why I like selling put options. There are cases where I will buy the stock outright, such as if the company pays an attractive dividend, is the potential target of an acquisition, or if I predict the stock will appreciate considerably. One downside of selling put options is that the put option seller does not receive dividends, because she does not own the stock. But for companies that don't pay dividends, selling a put option is an attractive strategy.

What Happens at the Expiration Date?

Only two things can occur when the option expires—either the price of the stock is *above* the chosen strike price or it's *at or below* it. If the stock price closes above the strike price, then the trade is over and the option expires worthless. The option buyer walks away with nothing while the option seller gets to keep the upfront cash with no further obligations. If the stock price closes at or below the strike price at option expiration, the option buyer will likely "exercise" her right and you will end up having to buy stock you wanted at the price you wanted (the strike price), even if it is trading at a price below the one you wanted.

Rate of Return for Put Options Compared with Other Investments

Calculating my rate of return on the sale of a put option is just a bit more complicated than calculating my rate of return on the sale of stock or the purchase of an interest-generating vehicle like a CD or bond.

Example 1: When I buy stock and sell at a higher price, it's pretty simple to calculate my rate of return. Assume I buy 100 shares of NKE at $71.94 per share and sell them a month later at $73.15 per share. I would have made $121 on a $7,194 investment. The monthly return is approximately 1.7%. This return could be higher if a dividend is collected during the holding period.

Example 2: It is also easy to determine my return on a CD. Suppose I invest $7,000 in a CD that pays 2% interest over a 12-month period. At the end of the year, I will have received $140 in interest. My monthly rate of return is 0.17% (2% divided by 12) or $11.67. (Gosh, this is barely enough money to treat myself to a manicure.) In the case of the bond, in addition to the interest rate, I will need to factor in the price of the bond when I sell it. If I don't hold the bond to maturity, my sales price could be lower or higher than the initial price I paid for the bond.

Example 3: Just like a bond or CD generates income, I can calculate my return on the put option by dividing the amount of income (which is the premium) I receive by the amount of capital that was allocated to the possible stock purchase. I receive $121 in exchange for setting aside for 30 days $7,000 to potentially purchase stock. That's a 1.7% monthly return.

Compare examples #1 and #3. Both generate the same monthly return of 1.7%. However, in example #1, I only make that return if the stock goes up in price. In example #3, I have a *much higher probability of success* in making that return because the stock price can go up, stay flat, or even decline somewhat. Talk about having control over your money!

> I have a much higher probability of success in making that return because the stock price can go up, stay flat, or even decline somewhat. Talk about having control over your money!

What is so exciting about selling put options is that I can be as risky or conservative as I like. I can target higher returns by taking high risk or lower returns by taking lower risk. In the NKE example, I don't have to choose the 70 strike price. I can choose a strike price that is higher or lower. If I choose the 67.5 strike price, I get much less in premium—only $62 in this case. That is a more conservative choice, because I only have to take ownership of the stock if it falls all the way to $67.50 instead of $70. If I want to be more aggressive and I believe that NKE will be trading above $72.50 at expiration, I can choose the 72.50 strike price and get more in premium—$223. But in that case I will have to take ownership of the shares if the price doesn't rise to at least $72.50 and stay there at expiration.

What's the Catch?

There are two primary risks to selling put options:

1. Just like in the example of the stilettos in which you may have to pay $180 for shoes that have been marked down to $160, you are obligated to pay a higher price for the shares than the market price if the strike price to which you committed is

higher than the price of the stock at expiration (occasionally you get assigned the stock even before expiration).

2.   You don't get to participate in the upside if the stock soars in price. But how often do all your stock picks quickly soar in price after you buy them?

As I stated earlier, selling a put option is like getting paid immediate income to enter the near equivalent of a limit order on a stock you want to own. The maximum gain is capped at the premium you received for the sale of the option while the risk is similar to owning the stock, with one important difference. Because you received income for selling the put option, you have generated income to offset some or all of a drop in stock price. Your cost basis of the stock is effectively lowered. For me, the benefit of not missing out completely on profits via the premium received up front and the reduced downside risk outweigh the benefits of an occasional stock that rallies more than I expected.

Selling a Put Option is Like Selling Insurance

Another way to consider the strategy of selling put options is to compare it to car insurance. If you drive anything like I do, you have probably filed an insurance claim or two. Instead of paying $3,000 out of pocket when you get into an accident, you only have to pay a deductible, and the insurance company covers the rest of the damage. In the case of car insurance, the insurance company is taking on the risk that the car you own falls in value because of damage. Let's say you buy a new car for $20,000 and hit a pole driving out of the car dealer's lot. Now the car is worth less than what you paid for it. Unless you get it fixed, it is now worth $17,000.

Does this ever happen to a stock? Sure it does. Stocks drop for a variety of reasons, such as bad economic news or quarterly earnings announcements that don't meet Wall Street's expectations. Often large holders of a particular stock will purchase put options as protection or "insurance." They want to ensure that if anything happens that will cause the price of a stock to drop that they have protection from severe losses.

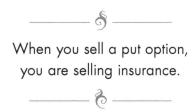

When you sell a put option,
you are selling insurance.

From where do these institutional or retail investors purchase their insurance? They purchase it from the put seller. When you sell a put option, you are selling insurance. Your car insurance company collects premiums for accepting the contract to cover the risks of those they insure. You act as the insurance underwriter when you sell puts.

If you are underwriting insurance and no claim is made against loss, then you keep the premium. If a claim happens to be made, you have to cover the damage; but you keep the premium, which should offset some (or all) of the payout amount.

In exchange for being paid a premium when selling a put option, you accept the downside risk of the underlying security. Insurance companies make billions of dollars annually because they know that most people are better drivers than I am and they are spreading that risk over a large population. Put sellers can also be paid for taking on those obligations in the stock market.

Please remember that no matter how attractive that premium payment, you must be ready and willing to purchase the stock if it falls in value. That's why it's important to want to buy the stock. In the worst case, you buy stock for a lower price than what it was trading at when you sold the put. You can buy your put option back if you change your mind and don't want to take ownership of the shares, but you might be in a situation where you have to pay more for the put than you got for selling it.

Selling Put Options as a Primary Investment Strategy

I certainly wish I had applied the put selling strategy to my investing toolbox years before I did. All those years I bought shares of stock and held them until they *finally* went up in price … what a waste of time and inefficient use of capital. Sure, many of the stocks did go up, and go up quickly. But what about those that grew at a snail's pace, or went up and down and never really went anywhere? And what about those that actually fell? I wish I had known someone like Emily back then.

When you hear the term "options trader," a female liberal arts professor is probably not the first image that comes to mind. Yet Emily sells put options as her primary investment strategy.

It was when Emily turned 30 that she realized she had to take control of her financial life. She recalls the bull market of the mid-to-late '90s when she started investing in the stock market. "At that point," she recalls, "you could be a monkey throwing darts at the *Wall Street Journal* stock page and make money." Sure enough, annual returns of the S&P 500 from 1995 through 1999 were at least 20% a year, and in two of those years over 30%.

Emily wanted to start investing in stocks and was referred to a stock broker. She was satisfied with the relationship until her broker recommended she purchase shares of WorldCom. The broker didn't sell even when it became clear WorldCom was a disaster. As WorldCom approached bankruptcy, Emily lost a lot of money. It was at that point that despite the strong urge to bury her head in a Jane Austen novel, she figured she'd be better off doing her own research.

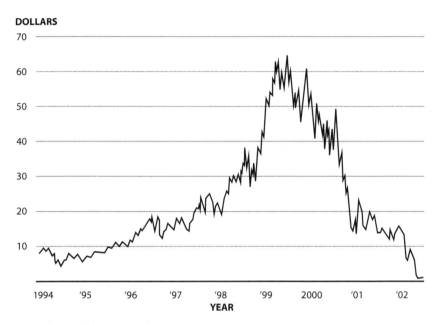

Figure 10: WorldCom stock price
Source: U.S. Securities and Exchange Commission

———— § ————

"You can't make money unless you
are willing to risk money."

Emily, liberal arts professor

———— ζ ————

Emily's experience with WorldCom taught her that she needed to diversify and rebalance her portfolio among various asset classes, but with equities still being the largest percentage. She explains that her money "isn't going to grow any other way if it doesn't include a significant stock piece." She adds, "You can't make money unless you are willing to risk money."

Emily refers to the system she has created for herself as "relatively simple and boring," adding that she believes women have the potential to become more successful investors than men because "they don't let their egos get involved."

Emily usually trades **blue-chip**, dividend-paying stocks and ETFs. She has between 20 and 25 stocks on her "watch list" and she knows their price patterns intimately. (I often instruct my self-directed clients to set up a watch list of five stocks and/or ETFs, each in a different industry sector or region for diversification, and get to know them like their best friends.) Emily uses **basic technical analysis**. When a stock falls near its **support** level, she'll sell a put with a strike price below the support level. If she is later "put" the stock (meaning that she has to purchase the stock at the strike price), she'll wait until the stock rebounds toward its **resistance** level and then sell a call option on it. If her stock gets called away, she'll take her capital and use it to sell a put on another stock that is trading near its support level. Just as during the 19th century society about which Jane Austen wrote, Emily observes that for many women, "It is cultural that their financial plan is a man." In Emily's case, a man is definitely not a component of her financial plan. After paying professionals to manage her money in the past, and being burned by the WorldCom scandal, Emily feels more confident doing her own research and managing her own portfolio. "Nobody has as much incentive as you do to see your portfolio grow.

> A company is considered **blue chip** if it is large, well-established, and financially sound, with a reputation for consistently paying dividends.

> **Technical analysis** is the study of trading and price history of a stock to forecast its future price. **Support** and **resistance** are considered important data points.

Many portfolio managers get paid no matter what sorts of returns their clients make. If you learn basic investment techniques, you can take pride in your own achievements."

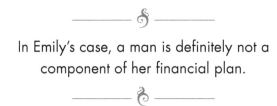

In Emily's case, a man is definitely not a
component of her financial plan.

Selling Puts to Profit from a Public Relations Disaster

If you practice yoga, no doubt you have heard of Lululemon (LULU).

At my San Diego health club, many of the ladies parade about in their trendy Lululemon gear. Even though I think the clothes are overpriced, I succumbed to "Lulu-lust" last year and bought two pairs of shorts and a gym bag.

Imagine my surprise on March 18, 2013, when I read the headline, "Lululemon Stock Drops Thanks to See-Through Pants Recall." I logged into my TD Ameritrade account and pulled up a chart of the stock price history for LULU—and I saw an opportunity to profit on the public relations disaster facing the company.

Let me cut to the chase: I made $695 in just two days by selling put options on LULU, and I am going to show you how I did it.[9]

I have been trading stocks for two decades, so I have found through experience that when unfortunate things happen to good companies, investors often overreact and unload the stock, which causes the price to drop temporarily. In many cases, the stock rebounds somewhat over time. But there are times, of course, when a stock will drop and never fully recover.

Being the frugal person I am, I rarely pay full price for clothes. If I see a $90 sweater I want to buy, I wait until it goes on sale. By selling put options, I do the same thing with stock I want to acquire.

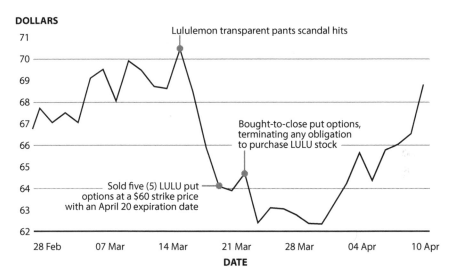

Figure 11: Selling put options after Lululemon's (LULU) see-through pants incident
Source: Price chart provided by TD Ameritrade

§

What did I get in exchange for entering into that deal? I received a premium of $1,100 in my account instantly.

§

As illustrated in **figure 11**, LULU was trading above $70 per share before the recall news hit. It plunged on March 18, and then opened up around $63 on March 19. On the 19th, I sold five LULU put options at a $60 strike price with an April 20 expiration date. In selling those put options, I entered into an obligation to purchase 500 shares of LULU stock at $60 per share on or before April 20. That meant that I needed $30,000 cash in my account ready and waiting to purchase those shares of stock should I be assigned the stock. What did I get in exchange for entering into that deal? I received a premium of $1,100 in my account instantly.

What happened next? That day, LULU's stock price began to rise. Not a lot, but in the right direction for my trade. Sometimes when a stock's share price is affected by bad news, it rebounds partially or fully over a short period of time, especially if the company indicates how it might correct the issue. Had the price stayed above $60 for the next month, the option would have expired and I would have kept the entire $1,100. But I'm a fairly conservative trader, so by the time I had made more than half of my maximum potential profit (which took all of two days), I executed a "buy-to-close" order and terminated my obligation to purchase any LULU stock.

> **Buy-to-Close** is a type of order commonly used in options trading.

Many factors affect the price of options, including the price of the underlying stock and the time to expiration. I was able to buy five put options at a lower price than I sold them for because the price of LULU shares started to rise, which was one of the factors that lowered the value of the put options.

As it turns out, my prediction that the company would assuage consumers about the recall of the see-through pants was right and the stock never dropped as low as $60. In fact, it resumed trading near the previous level of $70 only three weeks after the bad news report. But I don't care that I missed out on another potential $405 had I held the position to expiration. A good trader knows when to take gains and cut losses, and consistency of behavior is important.

Just remember that if you decide to sell one put option on a stock, you must be ready and willing to purchase 100 shares of stock at the price to which you committed, even if you end up overpaying because the stock dropped below that price. In this case I would have been happy to purchase the shares at $60 if they had been "put" to me. (Remember that I sold five put options, which obligated me to purchase 500 shares of stock at $60 per share.)

I thought about taking what's left of the $695 after taxes and loading up on LULU gear. But instead, I looked for another opportunity to buy stock on sale.

What I have covered in the past three chapters is technical and can be overwhelming when you are first exposed to the concepts. Please don't be intimidated. Women of all ages, whether they have computer expertise or not, can learn to apply these strategies on a regular basis. As you will read in the next chapter, even grandmas trade options!

Chapter 8

Even Grandmas Trade Options

WHEN I INFORMED MEN who work in the financial services industry that I was writing a book to encourage more women to trade options, I received a variety of reactions. Although some men who provide trading platforms or education to options traders cheered me on because I have the potential to grow their market, mostly I got the response that it will be "a tough sale." When I probed further, a few men came out with what they really thought: that *options trading is too complicated for women.*

> When I probed further, a few men came out
> with what they really thought: that *options
> trading is too complicated for women.*

Did these men think that women don't have the intellectual horsepower to understand and trade options? Perhaps they assumed that women aren't tech savvy enough to use the Internet to trade options? I enjoyed dispelling both myths at the same time with my zinger: "Did you know that even *grandmas* trade options?"

It's Never Too Late to Learn

Even in this day and age, women often defer to men on financial decisions. I was invited to speak at a women's "Health and Wealth" spa day, and the topic the organizer asked me to speak on was "Love & Money." This made me chuckle, because although I am an expert on *money*, both my husband and former psychotherapist would be the first people to state that I'm definitely not an expert on *love*. Nonetheless, that was the topic they gave me.

As I thought about it, I realized how the two topics—money and love—are so closely intertwined for women. In my research for this book, I asked a number of men who were married to educated and intelligent women, "Who in the household makes the decisions about money?" I have heard the following joke more times than I can handle: "I earn it and she spends it." Once I was lectured by a man about how he was the CEO and his wife was the COO of the household's finances. (In a corporate environment, a CEO typically focuses on policy and strategy while the COO focuses on implementation.) I said to him that I wasn't interested in who pays the bills; rather I wanted to know which one of them was charged with making the intellectually challenging decisions about how to invest and allocate their assets so they grow. He seemed stunned that I would even pose the question.

In fairness, many men have asked for my advice on how to help them convince their wives to take a more active role in portfolio management. One gentleman told me that since he was overweight and in poor health, he knew there was a high likelihood that he would die before his wife. It made him crazy to think that he would leave millions of dollars to his wife and she would fall in love with a con man who would take all her money. Apparently, that very thing happened to one of his wife's friends.

The bottom line is that you could be one of
the women ending up widowed or divorced.
That is why it is so imperative that you
understand how to manage your investments,
and it is *never too late to learn.*

In the United States women, on average, live five years longer than men. There is an often-quoted statistic that half of all marriages end in divorce. While it's not pleasant to think about, the bottom line is that you could be one of the women ending up widowed or divorced. That is why it is so imperative that you understand how to manage your investments, and it is *never too late to learn.*

Trading in Financial Advisors for Herself

During my spa-day presentation, I discussed why it was so important that women take an active role in managing their investments, whether they outsourced that function to a paid advisor or managed their finances themselves. I also explained a strategy for women who wanted to generate income from their stocks: covered calls. This appealed to the ladies, most of whom were in their 50s and 60s. After all, who doesn't want to learn how to generate supplemental income? A few months after the presentation, Barbara, 64, signed up for my three-month coaching program so she too could learn how to write covered calls.

I enjoy working with Barbara. Each time we meet, she brings her laptop with a picture of her cute little granddaughter as her screensaver. Barbara is a small-business owner and very savvy. She trades stocks and covered calls within her Roth IRA where most of her retirement assets are contained. The beauty of the Roth IRA is that she doesn't have to pay taxes on her growth or distributions. All the dividend and call option premium income she generates writing covered calls compounds tax-free.

The beauty of the Roth IRA is that she doesn't have to pay taxes on her growth or distributions. All the dividend and call option premium income she generates writing covered calls compounds tax-free.

Barbara's story is inspiring. Hailing from the Midwest and growing up in a conservative household, at 18 she was desperate to leave home, so she and a girlfriend hopped in a car and drove across the country to Southern California. It was the '60s, and Barbara was living an exciting life. Barbara fell in love and got married. Unfortunately, her husband wasn't good at earning, saving, or managing money. By the time she was in her early 40s, she was divorced, broke, lacking a college degree, and having to support a son who still lived at home. Amazingly, Barbara had the courage to go to school at night and earn her undergraduate degree in art along with peers who were two decades younger than she was. To earn money, she did odd jobs, started an art school, and sold or bartered her art.

Barbara applied for a job at an art gallery, and within a few years became the top salesperson in the country. She thinks she got her strong work ethic from her father, who was a self-made man. He had worked his way up in the auto industry. Barbara made a smart move at the gallery: she contributed as much as she could afford to her 401(k), and the gallery matched it.

About a decade ago Barbara started using a financial advisor to manage her money. He was using mutual funds, and she felt the performance wasn't very good. Then her CPA got his license to trade stocks, so she moved her money to him. During the 2008 crash, she lost a lot of money. To this day she is still angry that he did not use strategies that would have protected her against such a big loss.

Despite being over 60 years old with no previous trading experience, she decided to open an online brokerage account and trade stocks in her Roth IRA herself.

Despite being over 60 years old with no previous trading experience, Barbara decided to open an online brokerage account and trade stocks in her Roth IRA herself. She has been trading stocks on her own, and now I am teaching her how to trade covered calls.

Barbara's advice to women is, "Even if you are married, it is really important to have your own money, know how to invest money, and know how to teach your children about money." She encourages women to invest both in property and the stock market and have confidence that they can do it without a man.

This Wife Manages the Couple's Assets

For senior citizens, there is a good reason why the wife should consider taking primary responsibility for managing the couple's assets: she'll be in that position by default if she outlives her husband.

Elaine, 69, is a retired reading tutor. She contacted me because she had just started trading covered calls and was looking for some one-on-one coaching to accelerate her progress. In the past, she and her husband had relied on financial advisors, and they lost a lot of money in both the 2000–2002 and 2008 market downturns. Prior to 2007, Elaine and her husband had most of their assets invested in Canadian Master Limited Partnerships (MLPs) due to their relatively high yield versus bonds and other income-producing assets. However, when MLPs started falling in value right before the 2008 crash, Elaine switched advisors to one who was a prominent trader with a marquee national reputation. The portfolio he ran invested clients' assets in 50% domestic and 50% international equities, without any hedging mechanism (something that could have been achieved if the advisor had overlaid an options strategy). As her assets plummeted during 2008, she called to get answers to her questions. She was told to "stay the course." But since both she and her husband were retired, the hundreds of thousands of dollars in losses were nearly devastating. "I asked all the right questions and got the party line that was designed to keep my money," said Elaine.

Elaine recalls, "I was tired of losing money and I'm not stupid." She figured that if she was ultimately going to lose money, she could do that "without paying anyone." So she started to learn how to manage her and her husband's retirement assets herself.

Elaine is unusual among her peers in that she manages the investments for the couple, despite the fact that her husband is an engineer and good with numbers. Although Elaine does not have a finance background, she says she reads everything "that passes by my nose." She started reading books and investment newsletters. At first she didn't have the slightest idea of how to pick a stock. After reading "everything I could get my hands on," Elaine discovered that covered calls provide the flexibility that buying stocks alone lacks. "I wanted some cushion and I wanted some income."

"I wanted some cushion and I wanted some income."

Elaine, retired reading tutor

Elaine is currently deciding if she wants to continue managing the couple's assets or pay a money manager who specializes in covered calls. Although she pays only a few hundred dollars a year for a subscription service that suggests certain stocks as underlying assets and feels she is now fairly competent executing the strategy, she is not sure if she wants to continue committing the time required each month. She and her husband want to travel more often.

Nearing her 70th birthday, Elaine is acutely aware that she and her friends could be in the situation where their husbands don't make it home one night. She is prepared to handle the finances whatever might happen in the future and recommends that other older women learn to do the same.

So if you think you can't learn these skills just because you're a woman, or because you're too old, think again.

Chapter 9

Hire a Money Manager or Do It Yourself?

I CONSIDER MYSELF RARE among professional money managers because I believe that most people should hire *two* people to manage their assets: 1) a financial advisor, and 2) *themselves*.

Even if you have a financial advisor and are happy with the job he or she is doing, I believe there is tremendous value in learning how to invest on your own by opening an online brokerage account in which you personally manage some of your assets. No matter how large or small your account is, the exercise of being your own money manager gives you the foundation and experience to evaluate your current financial advisor's strategies against those who compete for your business.

Whether you choose to manage an account for a short period of time as a learning experience or continue to do it for the rest of your life, I believe this is one of the single most important acts you can take to reach financial empowerment, because you won't have to *rely* on a third party due to your own fear and ignorance. You will have the *choice* as to whether you outsource your money management or do some or all of it yourself.

As an example, while I choose to outsource the cleaning of my house, the fact of the matter is I am capable of doing it myself. I am not *dependent* on another person to clean my house, but I'd prefer to pay someone else in order to free up time for me to focus on other responsibilities. I do happen to manage a small portfolio of duties on my own, such as cooking, scrubbing dishes, and doing the laundry. I like to think of money management in a similar way.

Managing Her Portfolio Is Like Brushing Her Teeth

Debby, 42, a training consultant, would never dream of hiring anyone to manage her money. For her, it is part of her daily routine—sort of like brushing her teeth. "We grew up with the stock market," Debby explained. "Our cat was named 'Dow Jones.'" Debby's father set her and her brother up with $20,000 accounts when she turned 16 and her brother was 17. Her dad subscribed to the major business publications and she and her brother were expected to do their own research on which stocks to buy.

Debby's mother had inherited real estate, but had no interest in managing it. Despite their wealth, Debby's father thought it was important for his daughter to live below her means and learn to become financially independent. Debby is thankful for her father's efforts. And as a gay woman, she wouldn't consider falling back on a male partner for financial security in any case.

Debby started investing in stocks of companies she knew and liked. She would do her own research and was an early investor in Apple (AAPL). Based on her personal experience, she doesn't understand why anyone would pay a fee to a money manager for something they could do themselves. She is also surprised that many women do not invest their money in the stock market, emphasizing, "You lose money in the bank."

She Invested What He Didn't Spend

"I got married late in life, so I had lived many years supporting myself and relying on no one," said Theresa, a 57-year-old accountant. "I had socked away money in a 401(k) and an IRA and was fortunate to work for a company that provided stock options as part of my compensation package. After the company went public and my options vested, I brought quite a nest egg to the marriage, while my husband brought his medical school debt."

Even when her husband began earning substantial income as a doctor—far more than she was earning at the time—Theresa continued living frugally, while her husband thought nothing of dropping $3,000 on a case of wine. "He made the money and I invested what he didn't spend," Theresa chuckled. "I insisted on putting money every year into our daughters' college education accounts and I managed them. I had a track record of growing money."

About the time Theresa realized her marriage was unraveling, she became more active in learning new investment strategies. During the four years she and her husband were separated, her husband asked her to continue managing his money. "He knew I was good at it and he saved money by not having to pay a professional," explained Theresa. "I even paid him an allowance from the funds."

Theresa and her husband used a mediator to negotiate a divorce settlement. According to Theresa, "If you ask my ex-husband, he'll say he got screwed, but I thought it was fair. After all, I was the one who made all the decisions on how to invest and grow his money."

Advantages of Hiring a Financial Advisor

Many investors who are capable of managing their own money prefer to use a financial advisor for some or all of their assets. A professional can save you time, design asset allocation strategies for a large or complex portfolio, employ tools and techniques you may not feel confident using on your own, and most important, provide perspective and focus. The average investor often lacks the emotional discipline to make the best decisions at the right time, often buying high and selling low.

Some people pay a personal trainer to keep them on track even though they could work out on their own. A good financial advisor whom you trust will remind you of your objectives in spite of the day-to-day volatility in the market, keep you disciplined and accountable, and ensure your investment program is suitable for the long haul. Finding the right financial advisor can take some time but is well worth the effort. In chapter 11, I suggest questions you can ask prospective advisors as you interview them.

Time Is Money

Gretchen is a 37-year-old lawyer who is married with three children. Her issue isn't lack of interest but lack of time. "Managing my time is my biggest challenge, so if I can pay a professional to manage our money, I'm happy to do it."

It took Gretchen and her husband more than four years to agree on a financial advisor. Gretchen admits she is more risk-averse than her husband, so finding an advisor who could take into account the feelings of both members of the couple and facilitate a compromise was crucial. Although their advisor is based on the opposite coast, she uses screen-sharing software to review the couple's portfolio with them. Gretchen and her husband actually prefer that rather than going to an advisor's physical office, because both can schedule the conference during their lunch hour and never have to leave their respective desks.

"For me, the most eye-opening aspect of working with a financial advisor was how much money we needed to save, considering we both make good incomes," explained Gretchen. "I absolutely had no idea how much money we would need to invest in order to fund our children's education and our retirement."

A Real Eye-Opener: How Financial Advisors Get Paid

Shopping for a financial advisor is definitely less fun than shopping for a new pair of shoes, but infinitely more important. The problem is, very few people understand how advisors are compensated and why that matters.

When I was younger, I never even considered hiring a financial advisor, nor did anyone ever solicit me. Besides, I was very happy with the job I was doing managing my own money. I used to travel a lot for work, and one day I was upgraded to first class and sat next to a man who said he managed the money of a local company's CEO, who I happened to know. Since the CEO was an intelligent and wealthy man, of course I listened to what this financial advisor (I'll refer to him as "Mr. Moustache") had to say. A few weeks later I ran into the CEO and asked him if it was true he used the guy I had met on the plane to manage his money. Yes, it was true, but he made sure to inform me that the advisor only managed *a portion* of his assets.

So I decided to give this advisor a try. After all, since he was managing a wealthy dude's money, he must be pretty good, right? I figured I would start with one of my smallest accounts, an IRA that had $32,143 in it. The mere fact that he accepted my small account should have tipped me off that he was more "salesperson" than "money manager." Advisors who build portfolios and actually manage your money typically have *minimum* asset levels of between $100,000 and $1,000,000. To expect that Mr. Moustache would actually take the time every month or quarter to pay attention to an account of my size was naïve.

I recall Mr. Moustache phoning me and telling me that based on his experience, splitting my money evenly among three different mutual funds would be the best course. He called this allocation his "special golden formula." He then explained the various "share classes" I could select, which I found confusing. The bottom line, as I understood it, is that I would have to pay fees through one of the following methods: 1) on the front end; 2) each year by realizing lower annual returns; or 3) on the back end when I wanted to pull my money out of the funds. He informed me that the longer I kept my money invested in the funds, the less I would have to pay in fees when I withdrew the money.

Mr. Moustache "managed" my account from April 2007 to January 2012, when I finally decided to transfer the money back to my online brokerage firm. In addition to being charged $45 each year for five years for the privilege of holding my IRA at his firm (a charge my online brokerage firm did not apply), I ended up with a little over $26,000 left in the account, which translated to a loss of nearly 19% over that nearly five-year period.

I invested my money with Mr. Moustache just six months before the market started to take a nosedive. Since he had no control over whether the market crashed or not, it wasn't the monetary loss I was upset about: it was his assertion that by spreading my assets across all three mutual funds I would be diversified. At the time I took his word for it without doing my own research. After I moved the money, I looked up the top ten holdings in each of the funds on www.finance. yahoo.com and discovered, shockingly, that each fund had significant overlap with the other two. All three had holdings in many of the same large-cap domestic and European stocks. That's some geographic diversification, but adding another fund or two—such as an ETF with exposure to companies in China or Latin America, or even commodities such as gold or silver—would have served me much better during that time period.

Why is diversification so important? Pretend you and I were partners in a restaurant and we had three desserts on the menu: 1) apple pie, 2) apple tart, and 3) apple strudel. Imagine one morning I ran into the restaurant and announced, "I'm sorry, but the barrel of apples we were going to use to make our desserts for the week fell off the back of my truck!" Investors who had all their money in domestic and European stock funds during that period were losing all their apples, while investors who also had money invested in other asset classes had something else to eat for dessert.

In addition to the lack of diversification, the expense ratio and other fees in these mutual funds significantly affected my returns and no doubt left me with a greater loss than if I had invested my money in lower-cost mutual funds or ETFs. I decided to read the prospectus for each fund he had recommended, and was stunned by the level of expenses and other fees. I recommend people read a mutual fund prospectus at least once in their lives. It is an eye-opener.

My experience motivated me to learn how financial advisors get compensated. Generally, there are four ways:

1. Commission only: There is no explicit charge for financial planning or investment advice. Recommendations consist of investments and financial products that have commissions or fees that often come out of your investment. Commissions can take any number of forms, such as a front-end sales load charged on a mutual fund, a sales commission on a non-publicly traded

> A **Real Estate Investment Trust (REIT)** owns income-producing real estate such as office buildings, hotels, or shopping centers.

> **Annuities** are typically offered by insurance companies and convert a lump-sum payment into a series of future income streams.

real estate investment trust (REIT), or a surrender charge imposed on an **annuity**. Sometimes commissions are paid directly to an advisor from an investment company.

2. Commissions and fees (also called "fee-based"): A fee is charged for financial planning or investment advice. Recommendations consist of investments and financial products that have commissions or fees that come out of your investment.

3. Salary: Incentives and awards are often provided in addition to salary when certain financial products are purchased based on the advisor's recommendations. Recommendations may also include investments and financial products that charge commissions or fees.

4. Fee-only: Fee-only financial advisors provide advice and/or ongoing portfolio management. A fee-only financial advisor cannot receive compensation from a brokerage firm, mutual fund company, insurance company, or from any other source than the client. One benefit of hiring fee-only financial advisors is that they have no financial stake in the recommendations they give you. They recommend only what they believe is in your best interest. (I am compensated by an "assets under management fee" as a financial advisor at Coastwise Capital Group.)

No one model is necessarily better or worse than the other. It depends on what products and services you need, your level of assets, how much you want to pay, and in what form you want to pay. For instance, if my client wants an insurance product, I cannot sell that to her. I specialize in investment management, and as a licensed investment advisor, have a fiduciary responsibility to construct portfolios that help my clients reach their financial objectives. A broker or "Registered Representative" is required only to recommend investments that are "suitable" for you. For example, most brokerage firms have no obligation to tell you that a less expensive version of an investment is available. They are allowed to put you in their own firm's S&P 500 fund even if a lower-cost ETF or mutual fund exists for you. In other words, a broker can legally put his own interests above yours when recommending investments; some do and some do not.

If you are interested in finding an advisor who can write covered calls in your account in order to generate income, reduce portfolio volatility, and provide downside protection, you most likely will need to select a firm that is a "Registered Investment Advisor" and builds portfolios using individual stocks and ETFs rather than mutual funds. These tend to be small, independent firms that are focused on building customized, in contrast to cookie-cutter, portfolios. At large brokerage firms, your advisor may actually be just a salesperson with the person or team managing your money many layers and thousands of miles removed. At boutique firms, the one actually monitoring your account on a regular basis is directly available to you.

When you hire a money manager you'll need to weigh a variety of factors, including investment strategies, expertise, cost, conflicts of interest, responsiveness to your needs, and trust. And whether it's *you* or someone you hire, remember that the important thing is that there is *someone* managing your finances. The time is now.

Chapter 10

Ladies, This Is *Our* Time

O VER THE PAST TWO DECADES, there have been countless personal finance books written by female authors for women readers. However, very few books have focused exclusively on investing in the stock market and even fewer on using option strategies to do so. Some may think I am "ahead of my time" by writing this book. On the contrary: Ladies, this is *our* time.

The Chaos of the Options Pits

In the summer of 1989, I was offered a paid internship with one of the hottest options market-making firms in Chicago. A pair of recruiters had come to my campus to recruit a Wharton undergraduate student. They had drawn a few undergraduate and graduate students from the most prestigious schools in the country, and I was the only female the firm selected that year. Although they had chosen me for my quick mathematical and statistical skills (I could do a lot of calculations in my head under pressure), once I arrived in Chicago, they assigned me to do analytical work for only a few hours a day: two hours in the early morning before the trading day started and one hour after it ended.

During most of the day, when I would stand around the trading pits assisting my superiors by communicating the bid and ask prices with my hands and shouting out orders that needed to be filled, male traders and clerks from our competitors would throw chewed bubble gum "bombs" at me. (In fairness, I think they threw them at everyone.) Everyone chewed bubble gum, because since you were discouraged from leaving the floor to take a bathroom break, no one drank water. I get thirsty just remembering it.

I had a fun time in Chicago that summer (mostly because I was 20 with a fake I.D.), but concluded that the options trading business was too chaotic and exhausting and not a good fit for me. It wouldn't be until more than 20 years later that I would trade options *for myself.* I never lost my passion for options, but until the past few years, trading them was not something that was easy or accessible for me or the average retail investor to do. The Internet and the robust competition among online brokerage firms changed all that.

Money Creates Influence

My motivation for building my wealth myself was so that I would never end up financially dependent on another person. For Liz Lemesevski, 46, her motivation was to create influence. Liz left a 20-year career working as a professional investor for high net worth individuals and pension funds to launch *Money Native*, a money-coaching business. Liz views money not as something to spend, but as a resource and means to achieve higher goals. She helps groom women to become leaders in their communities by teaching them how to have a "portfolio management" view of their personal and business finances. "For women to become leaders, they must understand how to attract investment dollars to their ventures," according to Liz. "If you have money and direct it with intention and stay involved, you can create influence.

You have options and improved negotiating power. You don't have to accept every opportunity that is given to you."

Liz and I met at Hera Hub (a work, meeting, and event space for women entrepreneurs) where we collaborate with other women who left their previous careers—either voluntarily or forcibly—to start their own businesses. Never before has there been a time when so many women have launched out on their own to create new business ventures. If these women don't understand how to manage their own investment capital, how are they going to be able to successfully attract and manage investment capital from others?

Finally the time has arrived when women are now able to benefit from the convergence of female advancement and the exponential growth of the Internet to become successful and empowered investors.

The Selectric Era

Of all the interviews I conducted for this book, the one with Chris, a 65-year-old retired respiratory therapist, was most significant to me. It was her story that reinforced my belief that publishing this book could allow me to become the female mentor that thousands of women my age and older never had.

Chris got a job as a secretary with a regional brokerage firm in 1969, the year after I was born. She was attending community college at night, where she learned about computers. Since no one at the firm knew how to use them, as they entered the mainstream she became invaluable and worked her way up to becoming a mutual fund manager. Then she got her *own* secretary.

Chris recalls that out of the 75 stockbrokers at the firm, none were women. When she expressed interest in getting her Series 7 license in order to become a stockbroker, the men discouraged her and told her she would never pass the exam. But pass she did and the men didn't like it ... especially her boss. "He didn't care about me or my advancement in the company," said Chris. "He was having an affair with his secretary and they were out of the office most of the time."

She started writing covered calls for income and actually earned more from her covered call writing than she did from her salary!

Soon after passing the Series 7 exam, she came in to work on a Friday and was told that on Saturday morning she would need to take an insurance exam. When she asked her boss why he hadn't informed her, he apologized and said he thought he had. The men in her firm were amazed when she passed that exam as well. "I was on a mission after that," said Chris. "At that point in time, there were several secretaries with college degrees who wanted to take the Series 7 exam. I mentored them, and they all passed," a proud Chris explained to me.

When Chris took the Series 7 exam, it was the first year questions on options were included. Without a mentor, she started writing covered calls for income and actually earned more from her covered call writing than she did from her salary!

Eventually, Chris was fired without a reason. A few years later she learned that her boss was having an affair with *her* secretary and she wanted Chris' job. So Chris started a second career as a respiratory therapist and began investing in real estate. Now she is back to writing covered calls and has taught her husband everything he knows about investing. Looking back, she is amazed that she started building portfolios on an IBM Selectric typewriter and is now trading covered calls on an Android phone.

Pantyhose and Lipstick

Vanessa, a 41-year-old interior decorator, got her first job in finance five years after I did. Like Chris and I, she lacked a female mentor and became discouraged with the finance industry. During the seven years she worked as a sales assistant at three different brokerage firms, she was reprimanded when she neglected to wear pantyhose and lipstick to the office. One of her jobs was to mail the account statements to clients each month. As she watched the clients get wealthier, she also noticed the brokers' commission checks getting heftier. None of the men took an interest in mentoring her to become a stockbroker, and she didn't feel comfortable asking the one female broker in the office, whom she found aggressive, abrasive, competitive, and not at all feminine. She left the industry after concluding there was no place for her as a feminine woman. She became an interior designer.

Last year Vanessa asked me to teach her how to trade stocks and covered calls. Achieving a high annual return wasn't her priority; she says she came to me because, after spending seven years assisting men to become successful, she felt, "I should know how this works."

After our first coaching session, she and her husband decided to hire me and my colleagues at Coastwise Capital Group to manage their investment portfolio, as they had both started businesses and wanted us to generate monthly income they could withdraw for living expenses by writing covered calls. At the same time, Vanessa opened a trading account with $10,000 and decided to invest in socially and environmentally responsible companies about which she feels passionate, such as Tesla.

"I'm not in a position to buy a Tesla car right now, but I can buy a few shares of stock," said Vanessa, who feels strongly that society needs to move rapidly to electric-powered vehicles. She bought ten shares of TSLA at $51.90 per share and has continued to invest in companies she believes will have a societal impact, including biotech and drug companies. She uses her iPhone to track the prices of the stocks she owns and those on her watch list.

Thinking back to her days as a sales assistant, Vanessa never dreamed that she would ever acquire the knowledge and experience to profit from the stock market, never mind trading from a mobile phone! She feels proud and empowered, and is married to a man who supports her journey.

Seize the Day!

I hope you can see yourself in one or more of the women I interviewed for this book. Whether you decide to open a trading account for the first time, add options to your stock-investing repertoire, increase your 401(k) contribution, or search for a new financial advisor, *now* is the time to act. Every step, no matter how small, will bring you closer to financial independence and empowerment. In the next chapter, I provide you with a guide on how to get started.

Chapter 11

Get Started

WHETHER YOU CHOOSE TO manage your assets on your own or hire a financial advisor, be sure to subscribe to the free monthly newsletter at www.theoptionslady.com featuring my assessment of the market, notices of classes and webinars, and helpful articles and videos on investing and personal finance.

Manage Your Assets Yourself

Want to start trading options? You'll need to do a few things to get started:

1. Complete an online trading account application. Although there are several good online brokers, my personal favorite is TD Ameritrade. You can find the online account application by clicking the "Resources" tab at www.theoptionslady.com. You'll need to determine what type of account you want to open. During the application process you'll be prompted with definitions of the various types of accounts. You can trade covered calls and cash-secured puts in either a standard brokerage account or an IRA.

2. Fund your account with cash or transfer assets from an existing account.
   - If you have a 401(k), 403(b), or similar retirement plan from an old employer, you can generally transfer the assets into a Rollover IRA.
   - If your income falls within certain guidelines, consider opening a Roth IRA with a deposit of up to $5,500 for 2014 ($6,500 if you are 50 and older).[10]
   - Regardless of what type of account you open, in order to be able to write covered calls or sell cash-secured puts, you'll probably want to fund your account with a minimum of $5,000. Even at that level, you'll be limited to the universe of stocks and ETFs with a price lower than $50 per share in order to write one covered call or sell one cash-secured put option.
3. Request Tier I options authority to write covered calls and sell cash-secured puts. You can either request this during the account application process or once your account is already funded.
4. Download TD Ameritrade's thinkorswim® platform and launch the paperMoney® account[11] if you want to practice before trading real money. Consult the free tutorials to learn how to use the platform.
5. Research stocks and ETFs by using screeners and analysts' research reports offered by your online brokerage firm, or check out some of my favorite sites[12]:
   - American Association of Individual Investors (aaii.com)
   - Better Investing (betterinvesting.org)
   - Dividata (dividata.com)

- ETF Database (etfdb.com)
- Investopedia (Investopedia.com)
- Investor's Business Daily (investors.com)
- Seeking Alpha (seekingalpha.com)
- StockScouter (money.msn.com/investing/stockscouter-stock-ratings.aspx)
- StockTwits (stocktwits.com)
- The Motley Fool (fool.com)
- Yahoo Finance (finance.yahoo.com)

6. Hone your covered-call trading skills by reading tutorials and watching videos at these sites:
   - Born to Sell (borntosell.com)
   - The Blue Collar Investor (thebluecollarinvestor.com)
   - The Options Industry Council (optionseducation.org)

Hire a Professional Money Manager

If you prefer to hire a professional to manage some of your assets, consider asking the following questions as you are interviewing advisors:

A. How are you compensated?

B. How do your fees compare with other advisors?

C. What is your account minimum?

D. Why should I choose you?

E. Do you personally own the same investment or insurance products you'll be recommending to me?

F. Do you use options to manage risk in a portfolio? If not, what techniques do you use?

G. What is your investment strategy in a bull market, flat market, and bear market?

H. If you recommend bonds or bond funds, what will be the impact of rising interest rates?

I. How often will you rebalance my portfolio?

J. How often will we communicate?

Endnotes

Introduction
[1] www.prudential.com/media/managed/Pru_Women_Study.pdf

Chapter 2
[2] http://www.jumbocdinvestments.com/historicalcdrates.htm

[3] www.financeandinvestments.blogspot.com

[4] This is the 25-year historical average annual return; individual year returns have been both higher and lower.

[5] Past performance is not a guarantee of future performance.

Chapter 5
[6] Scott Kyle, *The Power Curve: Smart Investing Using Dividends, Options, and the Magic of Compounding* (Sunbelt Publications, 2008), 44.

Chapter 6
[7] Kyle, *The Power Curve*, 151.

Chapter 7
[8] The analysis would change slightly if NKE were to pay a dividend to a shareholder during that period.

[9] This is not a recommendation to buy or sell LULU stock or options.

Chapter 11

[10] Go to www.irs.gov/Retirement-Plans/Roth-IRAs or consult a tax professional for advice specific to your personal situation.

[11] The paperMoney application is for educational purposes only. Successful virtual trading during one time period does not guarantee successful investing of actual funds during a later time period, as market conditions change continuously.

[12] The third-party sites listed in this chapter are not intended to provide tax, legal, or investment advice and should not be construed as an offer to sell, a solicitation of an offer to buy, or a recommendation for any security by the author, Laurie Itkin, or The Options Lady. You alone are solely responsible for determining whether any investment, security, or strategy, or any other product or service, is appropriate or suitable for you based on your investment objectives and personal and financial situation.

Glossary

Annuity: Product typically offered by an insurance company that converts a lump sum payment into a series of future income streams.

At-the-Money (ATM): Used to describe a call or put option that has a strike price equal to or near the price of the underlying security.

Bear Market: A market condition in which prices are falling for an extended period of time.

Blue Chip: Type of stock that is typically an industry leader, financially sound, and often increases its dividend over time.

Bond: A debt instrument typically characterized by fixed, semi-annual interest payments and a specified maturity date.

Bull Market: A market condition in which prices are rising for an extended period of time, often accompanied by optimism, investor confidence, and expectations that strong results will continue.

Buy-to-Close: A type of order commonly used in options trading.

Call Option: Gives the buyer the right (but not the obligation) to buy 100 shares of an underlying security at a fixed price before a specified expiration date.

Cash-Secured Put Option: The seller of such an option receives a premium in exchange for keeping cash available to potentially purchase 100 shares of stock at a fixed price.

Certificate of Deposit (CD): Pays interest slightly higher than a savings account and usually has a fixed term and interest rate.

Correction: A reverse movement of at least 10% in a stock, bond, commodity, or index which is usually short-term in nature.

Cost Basis: Price of an asset which is used to determine the profit or loss when it is sold.

Covered Call Writing: A method for generating additional income from a stock beyond what would otherwise be provided from dividends.

Diversification: A technique that reduces risk by allocating investments among various assets. A portfolio of different kinds of investments may yield higher returns and pose lower risk than investing in just one asset.

Dividend: A payout to shareholders, generally on a quarterly basis.

Dollar-Cost Averaging: Buying a fixed dollar amount of a particular investment on a regular schedule, regardless of the share price.

Equity: Ownership interest held by shareholders in a corporation; one of the principal asset classes and another term for stock.

Exchange-Traded Fund (ETF): A "basket" of securities (typically stocks, bonds, or commodities) that track a certain index, industry, or geographical sector, and is traded on an exchange.

FINRA: Financial Industry Regulatory Authority (FINRA) is a not-for-profit organization created by Congress to protect investors by making sure the securities industry operates fairly and honestly.

Fundamental Analysis: Method of evaluating a security that attempts to measure its intrinsic value by examining macroeconomic factors and company-specific factors such as financial condition and management.

Hedge: Entering a position that reduces the exposure or risk of an underlying position.

In-the-Money (ITM): Used to describe a call option with a strike price that is less (or more in the case of a put) than the price of the underlying asset.

Index Fund: Fund that attempts to track the performance of a particular stock or bond index by holding most or all of the securities that are included in that index, such as the S&P 500.

Individual Retirement Account (IRA): Provides tax advantages for saving for retirement and more investment choices compared to an employer-sponsored retirement plan.

Limit Order: An order placed to buy or sell a set number of shares or contracts at a specific price or better.

Mutual Fund: Investment vehicle consisting of a pool of funds collected from many investors for the purpose of investing in securities such as stocks, bonds, and money market instruments.

Option Chain: A matrix that traders use to find the premium for options based on expiration dates and strike prices.

Out-of-the-Money (OTM): Used to describe a call option with a strike price that is more (or less in the case of a put) than the price of the underlying asset.

Premium: The price at which an option trades.

Prospectus: A mutual fund prospectus contains details on its objectives, investment strategies, risks, performance, distribution policy, fees and expenses, and fund management.

Put Option: Gives the buyer the right (but not the obligation) to sell 100 shares of an underlying security at a fixed price before a specified expiration date.

Rate of Return: The amount of money made divided by the capital deployed for a given investment.

Real Estate Investment Trust (REIT): A financial intermediary that invests its equity capital and debt in income-producing real estate and mortgages.

Resistance: A price level that a stock seldom surpasses.

Rollover IRA: Type of retirement account in which an investor moves retirement savings from a 401(k), 403(b), or similar employer-provided plan while keeping savings tax-deferred.

Roth IRA: Type of retirement account in which an investor makes after-tax contributions. Withdrawals after age 59½ are tax-free, but contributions (not investment earnings) can be withdrawn without penalty before retirement because income tax has already been assessed on that money.

S&P 500: Commonly followed stock market index based on the market capitalizations of 500 large companies.

Securities: Financing and investment instruments bought and sold in financial markets, such as stocks, bonds, and options.

Stock Option: A contract that gives the buyer the right to buy or sell 100 shares of stock (or ETF) within a certain period of time at a pre-established price.

Strike Price: The exercise price at which the owner of a call option can purchase the underlying security or the owner of a put option can sell the underlying security.

Support: A price level through which a stock seldom falls.

Technical Analysis: Method of evaluating securities by analyzing market activity and trends such as past prices and trading volume.

Thrift Savings Plan: Retirement savings and investment plan for federal employees and members of the uniformed services.

Uniform Transfer to Minors Act: Provides a mechanism by which gifts can be made to a minor, with a custodian managing the assets until the child reaches legal adult age.

Volatility: The measure of the amount by which an underlying security is expected to fluctuate in a given period.

Yield: Dividends paid for the previous twelve months divided by the current price, expressed as a percentage.

About the Author

LAURIE ITKIN IS THE FOUNDER of The Options Lady and a financial advisor at Coastwise Capital Group, a boutique money management firm in Southern California.

Ms. Itkin launched The Options Lady to educate and empower women of all ages to take control of their money, become successful investors, and grow the money they work so hard to earn. She specializes in teaching conservative options strategies to generate income and reduce risk when investing in the stock market. She also provides professional money management for clients without the time or inclination to manage their own portfolios.

Ms. Itkin frequently appears on broadcast media as a stock market and personal finance expert. She is a regular contributor to *DailyWorth* and *Stilettos on the Glass Ceiling,* and has been quoted by *CNBC, MSN Money, CBS Money Watch, LearnVest, Investopedia,* and the *College Investor.*

Ms. Itkin has a B.S. in economics with a concentration in finance from the Wharton School of the University of Pennsylvania and holds the Series 65 license for investment advisors.

Ms. Itkin enjoys playing squash and practicing yoga. She lives in San Diego with her husband and stepdaughter.

Subscribe to The Options Lady's free monthly
newsletter by clicking on the subscription link at
www.theoptionslady.com.

"Like" The Options Lady on Facebook by going to
www.facebook.com/TheOptionsLady.

Inquire about professional money management
or individualized investment coaching by sending
a request to laurie@theoptionslady.com.

Book Laurie Itkin for your next seminar or
conference by sending a request to
laurie@theoptionslady.com.

Additional copies of
Every Woman Should Know Her Options
can be ordered at
www.theoptionslady.com.

Notes

Notes

Notes

Notes

Notes

Notes

Notes

❧ Notes ❧

Notes

Notes

Notes

Made in the USA
San Bernardino, CA
15 February 2019